T0312020

John Locke and the Bank of England

John Locke was one of the first shareholders of the Bank of England and participated in parliamentary debates surrounding its creation. He had a key role in the monetary reform of 1696. This book examines Locke's thought in relation to credit, banking regulation, the monetary and financial system, the gold standard and the principles of Natural Right. It also establishes a link between Locke's economic and financial ideas and his political philosophy.

John Locke and the Bank of England will be of interest to advanced students and researchers of central banking, financial history, the history of economic thought and political economy.

Claude Roche is special advisor to the President Rector of the Catholic University of Lille. He began his career as a management consultant, specialising in the area of collective intelligence. In 2010, he joined the Catholic University and resumed his PhD thesis work, devoting himself to Locke's economic thought.

Routledge Studies in the History of Economics

For more information about this series, please visit www.routledge.com/series/SE0341

John Locke and the Bank of England

Claude Roche

Translated by
Carl Pitchford

Routledge
Taylor & Francis Group

LONDON AND NEW YORK

First published 2021
by Routledge
2 Park Square, Milton Park, Abingdon, Oxon OX14 4RN

and by Routledge
52 Vanderbilt Avenue, New York, NY 10017

Routledge is an imprint of the Taylor & Francis Group, an Informa business

British Library Cataloguing-in-Publication Data
A catalogue record for this book is available from the British Library

Library of Congress Cataloging-in-Publication Data
Names: Roche, Claude, 1951– author.
Title: John Locke and the Bank of England / by Claude Roche;
translated by Carl Pitchford.
Description: Abingdon, Oxon; New York, NY: Routledge, 2021. |
Series: Routledge studies in the history of economics |
Includes bibliographical references and index.
Subjects: LCSH: Locke, John, 1632–1704. | Bank of England. |
Banks and banking–Great Britain–History–17th century. |
Economics–Great Britain–History–17th century. |
Finance–Great Britain–History–17th century.
Classification: LCC HG2994 .R697 2021 (print) |
LCC HG2994 (ebook) | DDC 332.1/1094209032–dc23
LC record available at https://lccn.loc.gov/2020053036
LC ebook record available at https://lccn.loc.gov/2020053037

ISBN: 978-0-367-85919-0 (hbk)
ISBN: 978-0-367-77618-3 (pbk)
ISBN: 978-1-003-01962-6 (ebk)

Typeset in Bembo
by Newgen Publishing UK

Contents

Preface

The first steps of our democracies took place in England at the end of the 17th century. They concerned the State's relationship with what the French would call 'le monde de l'Argent': in less than 10 years, it is indeed the entire way of financing the State that has been changed, but also, and even more so, the way money was managed, including the organisation of the financial system. Learned scholars speak of a revolution – the 'financial' one – that took place around the Bank of England.

Obviously, there is a paradox in seeing the English State – the model of liberalism – getting so involved in what was, in fact, the invention of monetary and financial *regulation*.

Yet, no doubt this has long inhibited reflection on the subject. It is only recently that research has become interested in the political action linked to this revolution: the question most often asked is that of its lines of force and, above all, its links to democracy. The work of North and Weingast can, in particular, be mentioned.

But, without wanting to criticise them, a very different point will be made here with focus on the *intellectual* issues surrounding these events. For if it is true that politics 'made' the financial revolution, then the principles and ideas that guided it – even though hesitantly – must be broached. They too helped to shape political action.

In this specific case, this refers to a great philosopher.

For it is well known that Locke played a major role in this revolution. In close proximity to the leaders and even first shareholder of the Bank of England – it is to him that we owe this monetary reform that formed the apex of these events. So, the question arises naturally of his contribution. Was he not one of the founding fathers of our democracies?

Such an issue is totally relevant today, perhaps even more so than ever.

For Locke's action has, of course, been widely discussed. Surprisingly, however, this was almost always done in solely economic terms – and more often than not – attributing the economic policies of his successors to him. In fact, and according to his main interpreters, he would only have pleaded for the withdrawal of the State from these monetary and financial matters. So, as if the political philosopher had put himself on the back burner regarding these issues.

Fortunately, this judgement is now being contested — Caffentzis is to be thanked for that — it is now question of his 'philosophy of money'. However, understanding Locke's contribution requires more than this mere observation. The purpose of this essay is to provide a substantive response.

Since the system that was created with Locke has unravelled before our very eyes in recent years, the priority now is to measure it.

Introduction

Locke is undoubtedly the most discussed philosopher in the academic world and not only in the sphere of philosophy. He is still being published about today; indeed, there is even said to be a 'Locke industry'. But, if he is so much talked about, it has as a lot to do with his personal action as with his philosophical writings. For Locke was not only the well-known philosopher – the father of the Enlightenment and the founder of political liberalism. He also played a major role in the life of his country, intimately linked to the power that emerged from the constitutional revolution. Though, the question often asked is about the meaning of this action: what does it have to do with his own philosophy?

It is, of course, beyond the scope of this essay to address it in all its dimensions. But to investigate the most obscure one in the eyes of commentators, yet certainly the most significant.

For if Locke had such an influence during his lifetime, he did not have it as a politician, as is sometimes believed, but as an economist, and more precisely as a financial economist. This influence came during this founding episode which was the creation of the Bank of England, a major event in our economic history, also known as the 'financial revolution'. Locke was so deeply involved that this process could be described through the very steps he took. He was one, if not the only one, who persuaded the Houses to abandon the old financial policy – a matter of the legal lowering of interest – opening the door to alternative policies (1692). Again, he was one of those who supported 'the Bank' during the project phase, which was organised by Montague (1693); he who became one of the Bank's initial shareholders when it was set up (1694). He was also the one who advocated a new monetary policy focusing on the reliability of money and which became the gold standard in time (1695). Finally, he was the one who took the most unpopular decision on behalf of the government: to maintain parity with metal, as it guaranteed confidence in credit and money (1695/1696). He only took a back seat during the 1697 reform through which 'the Bank' acquired a privileged position which, in practice, it would continue to have. But, this was merely acknowledging the monopoly situation that had thus been created.

The list is long, and should speak for itself. It shows that this great philosopher, known for his major contribution to our institutions, and at a crucial moment, made the project of building what would become the model for Western Central Banks his own project. This is still challenging, to say the least. But in reality, it only accentuates the unease we feel about the way in which this action has been rendered. Or rather, the opposite. For if Locke's intervention in monetary affairs has been identified, it has very rarely been related to the financial stakes involved.[1] On the contrary, an awkward silence dominates the matter, mirroring Schumpeter, the specialist in the history of ideas or Appleby,[2] Locke's most frequently mentioned reader. But the same can be said of those rare authors who have tried to qualify his relationship with the Bank of England. Like Kelly,[3] his scientific editor, they left this relationship unrelated to its fundamental positions, be they monetary or even financial.

Thus, this essay is meant to fill that gap.

Obviously there are reasons for this. We will discover them first in Locke's interpretation, which has never produced any minimal consensus on his economic writings. It is well known. For example, the last few decades have called into question the only point on which there was agreement, namely, his allegedly 'metallist' conception of money. Quite rightly so, in fact, but the result is that Locke is still not well known as an economist. But, the main reason for this can be found elsewhere. It lies in the events as such that have brought about this 'financial revolution', and that it is difficult to restore as their political and economic dimensions have been mixed up.

Since the instinct in the face of such a 'revolution' is, of course, to read it in economic terms as well as in monetary and financial terms. This is how the Monetary Reform is often compared to the liberal policies deployed under the gold standard – often against Locke moreover. But, the essential point is missed by judging it in this way. Since this means disregard this idea that, in the 17th century, there were no *political rules* for the management of the financial sector, most often just being satisfied with legislating on interest. It was therefore necessary to *create* these rules, starting with those on money that would be guaranteed on metal and which would long be the basis of credit policies. But, this also applies to the Bank of England because its principle was very simple, for us contemporaries: to create a national credit space capable of enhancing savings. However, its originality was to do this backed by sovereign debt, then by the new money, thus restructuring the whole financial system around them.

In fact, in both cases, it was about the implementation of regulatory mechanisms and such a choice is by nature political. It is even institutional because it was a question of creating an *action framework* for the State. But it is also the origin of these interpretation difficulties: because it was such a success economically speaking that the spirit in which the Bank's foundations were laid has been forgotten. Do the concepts for describing it really exist?

But, if this has been the case, the image this 'revolution' portrays needs to be reconsidered. First of all, that entails sketching a more ambitious project than the mere setting up of a bank, even a national one. For it was a question, also when it was being created, of defining its relationship with the money and establishing confidence in both. Indeed, this refers to a 'monetary and financial system', whose foundations would have been laid, and whose famous 'banknote' – because it could be converted into cash – will be soon the standard bearer.

Above all, however, it devises an *intellectually* ambitious project.

1 The financial revolution thought challenge

What commands respect in these events is the place given to debate and theory in preparing these decisions. Horsefield, for example, speaks of about 60 banking projects,[4] and there were a hundred published writings on money. The Bank of England was debated for a long time. This means that questions were asked, which was rarely done afterwards, on financial policy issues, the function of banks, the role of the state, the nature of currency and even beyond.

All these topics lead back to Locke.

For if the reader is not an economist, it should be pointed out that these are the most complex questions in economic theory – questions that have stymied entire economic schools – starting with the famous Austrian one. Then imagine how difficult it was to grasp them when it was 'also' necessary to think about the political stakes involved. Wennerlind is not wrong when he says:

[I]ideas were constitutive of financial revolution[5].

This is why this question about the Bank of England is not a historical one in the sense of restoring the interplay of actors who created it, or Locke's personal relation with its officers. Actually, Locke had an outside view of the bank, sometimes critical of its management, but above all, polarised by the political decisions that would affect it – and these decisions would 'make' the Bank of England. So, the question to be asked is not to know who took these decisions, or how, but how they *were thought out*, what reasons were put forward, and on what concepts they were based.

This question still has to be answered.

With this in mind, it is difficult to remain indifferent to imagining that Locke actually accomplished this genuine work of thought. This is, at any rate, what this work intends to demonstrate. Since proof of that can be found in this proposition resulting from his main text – 'Some Considerations...' – which was also the conclusion of his address to the English Parliament:

> But when a kind of Monopoly -[banks]- by consent, has put this general Commodity into a few Hands, it may need regulation.
>
> (SC-103,104)

The way in which Locke approached the financial dimension – discussing the regulation of banks while his contemporaries were discussing interest – makes a very strong case. It means that he was able to conceptualise the economic function of a bank which is – if we agree with Keynes – to transform savings into investment. That also means he was able to define the political tools to make it happen. This is the meaning of the term 'regulation' and one understands the tribute that Keynes addressed to him:

> The great Locke...in his controversy with Petty...was...the first to express...interest in abstract terms.[6]

However, it also means that he was able to rethink this 'raw material' of credit which is money, and this is probably the most uneasy part of this discussion.

It must indeed be considered that there was a very limited vision of money at the time, because it was always confused with the *physical supports* being used: literally speaking and for all observers, money *was* the object used in exchange – metal coins or paper regardless here. Now if it is still possible to think about interest on such a limited basis, this is no longer the case with credit and even less so with its regulation. These notions are too sophisticated so as not to require a *specific* vision of money, which today would be described as *abstract*. This is the heart of the debate.

For if it is true that Locke was able to think about this banking regulation, then it means that he was able to overcome *this conceptual* difficulty. So, this is the thesis defended here: *that Locke was able to think about the main aspects of this financial revolution, probably for the first time in the history of ideas*. But, it is also that he did so as a philosopher, and with regard to the decisions that have been mentioned. For the difficulties were so great in conceptual terms, and the stakes were so high, that they could not be overcome without the help of philosophy.

This thesis is strong enough to support itself.

This is why the subject of this essay will be deliberately restricted to this single discussion and to the only explicit positions taken by Locke on these occasions. It is upheld in this work that they, indeed, anticipated and *perhaps authorised* the financial revolution. For this was then an *open debate* – like Kant's meaning – where the core focus was on the arguments used and their political consequences. Either during:

- The setting up of the Bank of England, the principles of which Locke would anticipate in his address: 'Some considerations on lowering the interest…of money' (Chapters 2 and 3).
- The monetary reform, the conceptual basis of which would be provided by Locke in his economic writings, but also in his 'Treatise of Government' (Chapter 5).
- The notorious refusal to 'raise the value of money' that he would justify in institutional terms in his 'Further considerations…' (Chapter 6).

Reference is made to the bibliographical note at the end of this work.

2 The methodical approach for this work

Unfortunately, there will be one particular difficulty that will tightly steer the approach to be followed in this work. It refers to the discipline known as the 'history of economic ideas', which covers the contribution of the major authors on these subjects. Yet, the progress being attributed to Locke is quite considerable, as can be seen. But, the disturbing reality which cannot be ignored is that, apart from Keynes, *no other* author has managed to devise the interpretation which has just been provided. Schumpeter – an expert reference on the subject – would judge Locke as an author of the past. Like Marx, he said nothing of his reports to the Bank of England, neither Blaug, nor even most of the other expert commentators. It must surely be acknowledged that this silence is intriguing.

How can this work be so far away from such authors on such points?

This essay, however, makes that possible for one reason related to the role of philosophy in economic thinking – in this case, Natural Right. This means to say, as has just been explained, that Locke approached these economic questions even as a *philosopher*. But this referred not only to the political recommendations he was able to make and the moral reasoning he put forward. This also referred to the theories and concepts on which he relied; even though economic, they were embedded in his philosophy. The example of money is quoted here where Locke thus lays the foundations:

> Mankind has made of gold and silver by consent the general pledges.
> (SC-31)

This proposal is clearly of Natural Right – this is the meaning of 'by consent' – and it provides an instant link with the monetary reform: metal is defined literally as the guarantee of money. It is, therefore, a normative position of money. However, it is insufficiently known that such an approach is rejected *in principle* by the economy itself. Here Schumpeter's position can be quoted, which speaks for itself:

> [T]hat philosophy [be able] to influence economic analysis…is one of the most important sources of pseudo-explanations of the economic analysis.[7]

That is exactly what is being contested. For this anti-philosophical prejudice, shared *ad nauseam* by his commentators, has somehow distorted the reading of Locke's economic thinking. That is why even today there is still an unwillingness to comprehend.

But reciprocally, this criticism will have its own demands. This signifies the need for a detailed illustration that Locke's recourse to philosophy was a necessity: it was because of these previously mentioned theoretical difficulties to imagine what banks and money were used for – more precisely, to understand that these notions were inaccessible without moral thinking.

So the approach will be as follows: the purpose of this work is to show how Locke's texts help to shed light on the main decisions of the 'financial revolution.' But before analysing them, it is important to look at these theoretical issues that so many economists faced. They are called *the problem of thought raised by the creation of the Bank of England* (Chapter 1), as it is argued that Locke's greatness is to have been able to *respond* to these difficulties. The plan will be clear once these difficulties have been explained.

Now is the time for the reader to judge.

Notes

1 These exceptions include De Smedt [2007], and above all Wennerlind [2011].
2 *'Locke, liberalism and natural law...'*, 1976.
3 *'Locke on money: introduction'*, 1991.
4 In *'British monetary experiments'*, 1960, p. 114.
5 In *'Casualties of credit'*, 2011, p. 7.
6 *'General theory of employment...'*, 1936, p. 342.
7 *'History of economic analysis'*, 1994, p. 32.

1 The problem of thought posed by the creation of the Bank of England

The purpose of this chapter is to understand the theoretical issues, but which are in reality problems of thought, that arose when the Bank of England, the first true financial institution of our modern times, was created. They will be seen especially in the credit function, but also in the functions and nature of money.

In doing so, the aim is not to rewrite the history of the Bank of England, in a way that is commonly understood, in other words, retracing the action of protagonists responsible for setting it up. For even if this bank was indeed born out of such actions, even if they are easily identifiable, the independent nature of their rationality must really be relativised. It was not independent of a specifically intellectual context in Skinner's sense [1988], that is to say, of data, concepts and even theories on which such actions could be founded. As is already known, however, this context was problematic as it was not adapted to the facts and the subjects that were being discussed. And it is this difficulty that needs to be addressed here.

Therefore, it is easy to imagine that such decisions were part of a factual diagnosis of the country's economic situation, and it is important to reconstruct that.

1.1 Background to the creation of the Bank of England

This will not be difficult, however, because at the time England's economic perspective was easily identifiable and its situation is also widely documented. Therefore, this can be presented succinctly and described in three points.

- England at that time could be seen as a country transforming itself into a market economy; however, its core activity was still based on agriculture, with a high level of tenant farming. Its social structure bore the mark of this, with the emergence of groups linked to markets – such as the trading community – but inserted into a society still structured by orders. We refer here to Macpherson's work on King's data.[1] Above all, it was a country that was growing economically, albeit very moderately since the Restoration, but clearly driven by commercial activity, especially foreign trade. This point was accepted by the ruling classes.

However, the problem with such situations, as we have learnt over time, is often financial. It is that they are accompanied by significant financial needs, which affect the banking system by calling into question its ability to meet them. It is from these very needs that the Bank of England was born. In this particular case, they were coupled with a very high level of State debt, estimated at 30% of the domestic product (1697)[2] – as opposed to 2.5% in 1688 – due partly to the war situation. From this point of view, the situation was really very delicate.

- For there was indeed a banking system, quite developed even, it was the characteristic of the trading nations in the 17th century. There was even significant growth in private savings, as noted by Child. But fundamentally, this system was disorganised and incapable of covering these needs, with three particular characteristics. (1) It consisted mainly of *deposit banks* and money-changers – the famous 'goldsmiths' – which were internationally open and led often complex activities, but frequently quite small, and with a rather exclusive approach to their clients as their debts were not easily transferable within other banks. This was also the case with State floating debt – the well-known tallies – which were not really discounted. (2) It was also extremely speculative and so poorly regulated that it hampered the development of the economy. The forms it took will be outlined in detail throughout this book. But more than just a long speech, this statement by Pepys – a senior Navy official – summed up perfectly their image in the eyes of the main decision-makers:

  I did despair…so long as we and the world must be subject to these bankers.[3]

(3) Finally, it gave priority to State financing, but at higher rates – 12% or even 14% (North[4]) – because of the negative image of the Treasury. 'The credit of the Nation is low', Paterson would say.[5] This contributed to the feeling of financial scarcity that almost all the protagonists, including Locke, would echo. These points form the backdrop for the coming debates.

- There was, in the end, a major monetary crisis which weighed negatively on the guarantees offered to creditors. Locke would talk about the *'disastrous state'* of money, but given its importance, it will be seen in detail in Chapter 4.

It should therefore come as no surprise that the period being discussed here was marked by major debates on these financial issues. That is what will occupy this work. However, two points that will help in positioning the very beginning of the Bank of England should be mentioned.

Firstly, the trigger effect of the parliamentary debate held on interest in early 1692 should be noted. By abandoning traditional policy which was to lower interest by law, but without another solution - it opened up the door to alternative financial policies. And it is no coincidence that it was soon followed by numerous projects for a National Bank. It can even be considered as raising the curtain on the Financial Revolution. Secondly, among these projects, the Land Bank of Barbon and Asgill should be mentioned, which followed the attempts of Chamberlen and Briscoe and would be the main competitor of the Bank of England.[6] In spite of its failure, it represented an alternative form of bank, advocating the issue of private monies – in this case monies based on physical capital (a private money at the time was *bearer note*). In this respect, it can be called a genuine model – the 'model of money creation' – even if it would remain essentially theoretical as indicated hereafter.[7] On the contrary, it sheds light on the Bank of England's choices.

It is undoubtedly in this excitement, more than in a bad economic climate, that the immediate origins of the Bank of England should be explored. However, what makes it original is both the specific nature of the project and the complexity of its implementation. These points now need to be examined.

1.1.1 A politico-economic logic of creation

The Bank of England was set up in 1694, two years after the parliamentary debate, by an act granting it a privilege to carry out banking activities. There is little doubt among historians about the specific interests that led to this. They all describe this project as the combination of two different viewpoints: that of the trading community, who were very consistent on this point, and that of a fraction of the 'whig' political power, who was extremely concerned about State funding. This link of interest between the Bank and the State will remain predominant.

But even if the bank was born in 1694, it can only be considered as an institution, even at an early stage, from 1697 onwards. For it was at that moment that it would receive, contractually, dual exclusive rights to large banking activities and issuing money. But it would then be the outcome of a long decision-making process, which lasted more than 5 years and which included, beyond that Parliamentary debate, the whole Monetary Reform of 1695/1696 which played a pivotal role in its development. Thus, this complexity, which is outlined in the box below, has a twofold consequence on the discussion here.

• First of all, it puts a stop from thinking about this creation process in *purely* political terms, as has recently been the case.

Several works are alluded to here which have defended the importance of state financing in these events by relativising the economic determinants for the creation of the Bank of England. First of all, Dickson can be quoted who remained satisfied with explaining it through the emergence of a *stable and efficient government*,[8] or North who established new institutions, and namely parliamentary control as the main explanatory factor for its success. But Carruthers [1999] could also be quoted, even others who will see it in competition between the political parties.

There is, of course, some truth in these explanations – namely, in that of North – because the Bank of England has been the main operator of sovereign debt and its success has been necessarily linked to the State's mastery of its own indebtedness. On the other hand, it should be counter-argued that the management of the monetary reform by favouring the economic principle of confidence in money has overturned the exclusively political nature of these analyses. This will be discussed further below.

• This suggests, however, that there was a coherence inherent in these measures, which could be qualified as politico-economic.

For even if they were each time partial decisions, they all contributed to giving the Bank of England the same *economic function,* which can be seen in its ability to direct savings towards business and/or the State. They should, therefore, have an *objective meaning*, which had to be at least partially mastered by the decision-makers. This is the key point, the fact that this had to be thought through, but the important part is certainly to know how.

The Bank of England's institutionalisation process

- The beginning of the Financial Revolution started with the House of Lords rejecting a law lowering the interest rate (1692).
- The project of the Bank appeared in 1693, following a quasi-call for projects managed by Montague, and including several informal discussions with England's leaders. Everything was due to Paterson.
- The Bank was finally created in 1694, through a law without specific considerations, and due to start in the summer once the capital was raised. It reached £1.2 million, immediately reloaned to the State at 8%. This bank would initially be seen as the bank of the trading community; however, Weber would describe it as a model of Protestant ethics.
- In mid-1695 Paterson was dismissed from his duties, apparently because of his too risky loan policy. After Sir Godfrey's untimely death, it was Lord Houblon who took over as Governor for a term lasting several years. He was reputedly close to Locke.
- At the beginning of 1695, the monetary reform process began which was strongly supported by the Bank of England. This was carried out in two phases, the first supported by a group of experts, with Locke being the most influential. The principle of the 'recoinage' of silver species would be determined in the Summer which was then suspended following the Treasury's intervention requesting an 'increase in the value of money'.
- This measure would then be refused following Locke's intervention (November 1695, then January 1696).
- At the same time, the 'Land Bank' was launched (April 1696) which was intended to be a private issuing bank. This bank would fail to raise its capital in June of 1696, following the implementation of the monetary reform. During this period, the Bank of England faced a 'run', but showed resilience due to a capital increase.
- In 1697, and according to some authors (Andreades): given the overly competitive state of the banknote market, the Bank of England obtained the first exclusive rights to issuance, within a stipulated framework in the text.
- The share price rose from level 100 to 103 at the end of 1698, down to 75 at the end of 1694, 60 in October 1696 and 89 at the end of 1697 (Rogers).

However, this cannot be done without measuring the fact that this creation was based on the logic of *financial regulation*, and this term is to be interpreted in its original meaning: the creation, through public means, of the optimal conditions for carrying out banking activities. The idea is essential here because it was Locke who first succeeded in conceptualising it. Yet it is still badly perceived in the debates on these subjects because of the recurring confusion between the monetary and financial aspects. These need to be clarified.

1.2 The Bank of England and the principle of financial regulation

It is indeed very commonplace to present the Bank of England's first steps by highlighting its role in the development of fiduciary money – what would long be called 'banknotes'. Particular emphasis is placed on the compensatory role banknotes played in the consolidation of the financial system in the 18th century. This is why the Bank of England is often presented as a continuation of the Bank of Amsterdam, or even an issuing institute. Consequently, Locke has been strongly criticised for his – real – cautiousness in this area.[9]

However, this is a superficial view.

For if it is true that 'the Bank' obtained this monetary mission, three years after its creation, this could only be achieved on the basis of financial mechanisms close to 'securitisation', and for which Locke himself provided the grounds (regarding Holland):

> For the Debt of the State…is look'd…as a safe Revenue…they buy it one of another…whether there be any Money in the publick Coffers
> (SC 110,111)

In fact, the mechanisms consisted of transferring debt onto the State or using them as guarantees for other debt, including this famous money. However, such an approach only made sense on the basis of a prior positioning of 'the Bank', and, therefore, of a function assigned to it, which went back to this idea of regulation.

1.2.1 Principles for the creation of the Bank of England

Three points can be mentioned to explain this.

- The choice of the banking model made by the leaders was, first of all, that of a credit bank. This was an explicit choice from the very project stage. It means that the model of money creation was knowingly rejected, which was strongly disparaged among the trading community,[10] and that an intermediation model was proposed instead in which the Bank would act as a mediator between the lender and the debtor – see the savers and entrepreneurs and/or the State investors. This is what Paterson would mean while defending the principle of the pre-eminence of metal for all operations – read: without any reference to physical assets:

All credit not founded on the universal species of gold and silver is impracticable

(Op. cit., p. 10)

Yet such a choice had the consequence of placing the Bank at the heart of the financial circuit, forcing a certain optimisation of this circuit, when the alternative choice would have led to a different posture: that of an aggressively competitive bank on the private money market, acting against public interest.

- The second point is the amount of the initial outlay, which has been estimated at almost 20% of the sovereign debt (22% of the budget). Thus, beyond the considerable support as shown by the figures – particularly from merchants – it was also a mean to assert a strong influence on the very conditions of this intermediation, making this idea of regulation potentially effective. In fact, this was what really happened according to the interest rate criterion: it dropped as soon as the Bank was created, and even significantly, according to certain documents of the time:

It was pointed out that the foundation of the bank had sharply reduced the discount on governments tallies.[11]

So, this was a coherent decision as it was a question of optimising money flows and directing savings to the nation's economy. This was, however, a difficult decision in relation to the intellectual problems that this posed. As this idea of intermediation was far from simple – theoretically at least – since the *function of credit* had to be thought about. But before tackling this point, a question arises here which will outline what was at stake in the monetary reform.

While it is true that the Bank had, de facto, given itself a regulatory mission, it had not done so publicly, but privately in the form of a 'mutualist' bank.[12] It was, Locke would say, a tradespeople bank, and it will be seen later that he was in favour of State regulation.[13] Thus, this was not a simple technical difference, and it could be objected that the private nature of the Bank could easily deviate from its purpose.

This was not the case, however, and this is where the third point comes in.

• This can be explained above all through the structuring of the bank's initial capital, that is, the repeated choice of alternating between its capital and sovereign debt. Indeed, this was an outspoken stroke of genius – even if Locke did propose an initial outline. For this surprising choice forced the bank to operate on an original basis at that time, using a 'paper' asset (composed of State receivables), whereas other banks did so on a physical basis, usually metal. Rogers would say in this regard that on the contrary to the Goldsmiths: 'the Bank never pretended [keep species] deposited...but take them for trading'.[14] The reader should bear this point in mind.

As this would have twofold consequences and it is difficult to believe that this was not somehow anticipated. (1) It commanded careful management to avoid going against client opinions,[15] and Locke was very cautious on this point. This prudence moreover probably explains the rather inelegant eviction of Paterson. (2) But on the other hand, this choice was to anticipate the monetary reform that followed and which the Bank strongly encouraged.

Unfortunately, this point is still misunderstood by many commentators, and this is probably due to the same confusion between the monetary and financial dimensions of such an institution. This needs to be explained.

1.2.2 The monetary reform of 1695/96

Indeed, the Reform to which Locke attached his name is very often considered to be a purely monetary reform. As technically speaking, it only consisted of recalling silver coins in order to make them trustworthy. So it seems to have been a non-financial issue, and this is still the understanding that dominates Locke's interpretation – see Wennerlind.[16] However, this view is erroneous for two reasons.

1. On the one hand, it overlooks the necessity for lending to be based on the reliability of *metallic cash*, which was still broadly used for payments; this was illustrated with Paterson. It is on this point that authors such as Aglietta insist:

> [T]he most important factor was the institution of a system in which
> a (private) bank issued a currency, trust in which was maintained by
> convertibility into a high quality metal currency.[17]

In fact, and from the point of view of the profession as a whole, it
became vital that the client – in this case savers – remained confident in
the security of their investments, which the monetary crisis threw into
doubt. Hence, the purpose of the monetary reform was to remedy this,
which explains its *institutional* logic: it is often seen as the origin of the
gold standard.

2. But, it also fails to consider the stakes involved in the choice of the
   par value of this operation (the par value is the key to equivalence
   between the unit of account and metal). For at the time, there was
   intense competition between the different means of payment – coins
   and paper – and, therefore, between the different banking models
   because of the structure of their assets. On that basis, the decision to
   carry out this operation *at par* should be read as *a financial* decision,
   not just a currency one, and one which was mainly in favour of the
   credit model.

But conversely, this raises the question of how this monetary choice
could have been thought out.

1.2.3 The institutionalisation of the Bank of England

Indeed, these Reform choices had this immediate effect on the Bank
of England of stabilising its situation, to the detriment of almost all its
competitors. Thus, the Land Bank would be condemned to failure practically one month after launching the Reform, when it was recognised
that the Goldsmiths would lose their positions on the sovereign debt
market. The effect of the Reform has been, therefore, to position the
Bank as the privileged intermediary between the State and the financial
system.

It is this point, the author believes, that explains why 'the Bank'
acquired its status as an institution so quickly. For it took less than a year
between the implementation of the recoinage and the first reform of
the Bank of England (1697) and the dual monopoly granted to it. The
principles of this Reform speak for themselves since they constituted of:

- The renewal of significant funding rounds with the State
  (£1 million).[18]

- In exchange for a very tough limit on interbank competition and a regulated monopoly on money issuance (convertible into national money).

They were temporary monopolies, it should be underlined, but history has shown that they would be sufficient to secure the Bank's status in the long term. They can, however, be discussed rapidly here. As, indeed, it was simply a question of recognising the role that the Bank of England played henceforth in the financial system and its link with the interests of the State. This cannot, therefore, be referred to as a major theoretical issue surrounding this reform, an explicit issue in any case, but rather to consider it as the logical culmination of a creation process.

But at the same time it sheds light on the intellectual role played by Locke. This now calls for some precision here.

1.3 Locke's intellectual role in the financial revolution

Indeed, it is acknowledged that Locke was, from the outset of these events, a staunch defender of the Bank of England. His letters bear witness to this, notably his exchanges with the MP Clarke.[19] And as such, he should be regarded as a political friend, with all that entails in terms of informal relations and mutual trust: he was close to some Bank's officials, particularly its future Governor, and would back it from the early stages. He was to become the first shareholder when the call for funding was launched, for a substantial sum − £500 then £600[20] - and most of his work as an expert would be in relation with the Bank, including on the Board of trade (Laslett [1957]). But he would also have his own view on its management, which will be discussed in the conclusion of this book. It reveals a certain reservation about the monopoly status it was to obtain. In any case, it is uncommon to see a philosopher so closely linked to the financial world.

However, it is important to take a step back and put these personal aspects into perspective.

The question being asked here is not about the protagonists who set up the Bank of England, even if they were philosophers. The question is more about the *decisions* that moulded this action and the debates they elicited. What needs to be examined, therefore, is not Locke's personal action, but his intellectual contribution to these decisions. For these measures required an original thought process that *only he* could have achieved. He did so actually, on three occasions which were formal debates supported by written material:

- At the time of this monetary reform, for which it is known that he provided the unofficial considerations. He even did so twice: before the reform and from within the group of experts, where he received the strongest support (1695), and when the money's par value was chosen (end of 1695).
- But he also did so prior to the creation of the Bank of England, notably during the first parliamentary debate on the financial question. It is worth emphasising this point.

It can actually be imagined that the process leading to the creation of the Bank of England began de facto during this session when a draft bill was contested then rejected – which was very current in the 17th century and would have prevented any initiative regarding this topic: that of lowering interest by law. It has been acknowledged, moreover, that it was Locke himself who fought against it. But, it must also be underlined that he achieved it through the alternative proposal to *regulate the banks*, an idea that was unheard of at the time, but whose significance is now taken for granted. Reiterating this point, Locke stated explicitly: 'banks may need Regulation'.

At the very least, this suggests that he had identified the role played by lending in the economy, which already provides a response to the criticism he received. Above all, it suggests that he had already anticipated from this moment the function that would be given to the Bank of England. If this is related to his influence on monetary reform, then this assumption cannot be avoided: that on these three occasions, *Locke succeeded in setting out the political and theoretical principles that led to the creation of the Bank of England*. This was not in any way complete, as was just mentioned, but he did enough to justify to policy-makers the exceptional role that would be assigned to it. Surely he would be the only one capable of doing this.

But here again, caution is advised regarding this proposal, and place it in the intellectual context of that time.

1.4 Thought issues related to the construction of the Bank of England

It needs to be recognised, indeed, that the hypothesis just put forward amounts to attributing a philosopher's thinking to a decisive role in these events: that of anticipating financial decisions that a political power should have taken. This is rather uncommon. Thus, it could be invoked here as having committed a sin of over-exaggeration or intellectual smartness, by ignoring the fact that the main protagonists themselves could propose such decisions. Moreover, most works on the history of the Bank of

England can be read along the same lines: they implicitly imply that these decisions were intuitive for those protagonists – in particular, Francis [1888], Clapham [1944] and even Rogers [2001].

However, an essential point of these events has been overlooked.

For to do so, it would have been necessary that the economic thinking of that time could have supported such measures, which signify the existence of theories capable of providing them with meaning. This is essential in the field of economics. Yet, it is well known that this thinking, even if already formalised, was rather weak at that time, particularly regarding the points discussed here. Historian–economists have even coined a term to describe it. They speak of 'mercantilist' thinking to emphasise the fact that these difficulties were common to almost all the authors of that time. See hereafter on the ambivalence of the term.[21]

What must be examined then is the nature of these difficulties as it is conversely from this angle that light will be shed on Locke's real contribution. They will be referred to as *the thought issues* linked to the creation of the Bank of England, and they will be dealt with gradually. It will also be necessary to identify the specific limits of Locke's interpretation.

1.4.1 The conceptualisation of credit and its function

1. There was a *theoretical problem*, first of all concerning credit and its function

The main point to consider is to recognise that the measures being discussed here were based on concepts that are certainly familiar to the reader, but which were extremely problematic at the time. For example, savings and investment, which theoretically delineate the function of the system that came into being with the Bank of England: these are macro-economic concepts, the meaning of which was largely unknown, and everyone can see that.

However, it was especially the notion of *credit* that was sensitive, and behind it the idea of its *function*. For a loan is an absolutely particular transaction. It is a contract, which cannot be thought of as an exchange or the product of a market. On the contrary, it can only be interpreted as an asymmetrical transaction linking two different uses of money: the *act* of lending, where money is transferred, and the *use* of the money lent, including interest. Through this use, moreover, the function of credit can be determined, which for Locke would be precisely to *transform the money saved into investment*. He shared this idea with Keynes. Now – and this is fundamental – this approach was not only ignored at the time, and this can also be confirmed, but *forbidden* to even consider. This was so for the simple reason that the theory could only represent exchanges of commodities or markets, which both refers to symmetrical transactions. In other words, economic theory was limited to only money circulation and reasoning about lending was only held by affinity with these models. The following is an example of such thinking:

> [T]he usury is merely a reflection of what is natural: the balance of forces in a market economy.[22]

From this point, observers were forced to adopt a restrictive approach, limiting lending to the sole supply and demand of money, or even to the sole logic of arbitrages. Moreover, it was impossible to theorise any relationship between interest and the real economy, through investment, for example.

> ==> This, therefore, refrained any acceptable thinking both about the *function of credit* and the *idea* of regulating it, while these were very significant issues.

These difficulties are generally condensed and referred to as 'monetary theories of interest'. This will be the first point.

This tension, should be pointed out, has been identified through the history of ideas, even if not fully understood. But how should it be measured? This history explains indeed that this 'monetary' approach was a major limitation for mercantilist theories, because it was to be found again in other topics such as capital. It is notably the case of Schumpeter,[23] who is the author of reference on these subjects. But, it also explains such unease for *monetary* reasons: because it was linked at that time to an archaic vision of money which was systematically confused with metal, or even capital. It is essentially this vision of money that explained the theoretical weaknesses of the mercantilists. Besides, this was one of the criticisms that aimed at Locke:

> Locke's confusion between money and capital [is] well known.[24]

Such an analysis, if Locke is set aside, is not unacceptable. For it is true that the origin of these theoretical difficulties lied in the concept of money. This analysis, however, is too superficial, because it ignores the *conceptual* nature of the problems raised by money, and for this reason, the diversity of theories of money that emerged at that time. It is essential to clarify these points.

1.4.2 The spectrum of money analysis – money as an object

The reference interpretation on these subjects is that monetary theory in the 17th century was largely dominated by a movement that it describes as mercantilist and/or metallist,[25] the latter being used for debates on money. This can be partially accepted. For it is true that the authors who participated in the long debate on interest in this century all agreed on this twofold belief: firstly, that money was comparable to metal and, secondly, that these metals were commercial goods singled out in the end by history. This is the definition of metallism – see Child:

> [We] sell out our commodities…for as much silver as ever…the merchant observing…the intrinsic value of money…not the name.[26]

It is fair to say, moreover, that this movement stretched a 'monetary approach' to interest since metal only transferred an exchange value on money. Mun, Culpeper, Child, and even North,[27] and also Petty[28] can be cited. But this monetary logic was also true for those more advanced theories that derived the value of money from its use in the market – even if it remained a commodity. Here Davenant,[29] and also Cary:

> [I]n formed societies…the worth of money [takes] his Rule from the necessity men have of other Commodities.

However, this judgement is no longer accurate in relation to works dedicated specifically to money, or even to new banking systems. On the contrary, it must be noted that particular movements have emerged out of these weaknesses and they must be understood as attempts to outmatch metallism, respectively:[30]

- Vaughan and his followers, for whom metal and money were defined as pledges and no longer as commodities:

  > The first invention of Money was of a pledge…for when men exchange…[and] both parties could no always fit one another at the present.
  >
  > (Op. cit., p. 1)

This was in reality a financial definition of money, since a pledge is the object that is placed as collateral for a loan. It would therefore have all the uses of money – see below on the notion of functions of money. But it remained de facto metallist because it still bore a confusion between metal and money.

- For the so-called Cartalist movement, money was no longer 'metal', but had to be considered as a 'voucher' in other words, a mere support with legal tender. On the other hand, this was an innovative standpoint because this legal tender gave the currency an 'extrinsic' value. It must even be considered as the very formulation of the money creation model, since according to these authors any private claim, endowed with legal tender, could become money. Consequently, Barbon, its main representative, should be mentioned in priority:

> For the Value arising from Publick Authority, it may as well be set to anything else that is as convenient'
>
> (Op. cit. p. 13)

Thus, Potter [2010], Law [1705] and also Lowndes[31] or Temple [1696] – in other words, Locke's most staunch opponents – can be cited here.

- Chapter 5 will focus on the jusnaturalist authors.

The monetary debate of that time cannot therefore simply be limited to pure metallism. However, what must be understood – and what the reference interpretation has lacked – is that even though they were innovative for their time, these movements remained limited concerning a key point in common with metallism:[32] the fact of seeing *money as material*, of considering it as an object, whether paper or metal. This was of course logical at that time. Nonetheless, this 'materialism' actually presented conceptual problems that defeated these movements. These problems could even be qualified as philosophical, which explains the silence of the historians of ideas.

1.4.3 The two monetary aporias of Locke's contemporaries

This can be quite easily appreciated, moreover, by going back over the requirements of a credit theory. This has just been noted, as such a theory would require a comparison between the lending transaction and the interest calculations, and this was a difficulty. But the important point now is that any attempt to overcome this situation – that is, to make a calculation on these terms – was hampered by the fact that these elements were of a different monetary nature and therefore heterogeneous: with interest being expressed through a debt – thus 'on paper' – whereas the loan was transferred 'in cash'. It should be noted, moreover, that this difficulty overlapped with the questions raised during the monetary reform. Such attempts encountred then…

2.   … an epistemological limit linked to the functions of money.

This can be explained as follows: in fact, the only way to make this comparison is based on the notion of *monetary functions* which are an abstraction from the notion of the use of money. It is argued then that money has such functions which are homogeneous and enable such a comparison: an intermediary exchange function, which is intuitive and a store of value function which reflects the promise of deferred payment linked to money – the details of which are outlined hereafter.[33]

The problem, however, is that these are abstractions, which *can only be made sense* of if money is thought of as *abstract*. This is easy to admit (money is abstract when it means an ideality like the 'euro'). But as has just been observed, these monetary movements retained a material vision of money, it was always an object for them. They confused money with these monetary supports '*there-in front*' according to Heidegger. They therefore balked on this 'invisible' difficulty which forced them to use only the notion of the *use of money*, making them incapable of theorising what they knew well in practice. Exactly so, they balked on the limits of this reality which is that the use of money is *necessarily unique* at a given moment – and only allowed them to theorise the uses linked to circulation. This was what Vaughan, the exception in this case, demonstrated 'a contrario'.[34] It was perhaps here that the weakness of Locke's contemporaries would be most noticeable. For,

> ==> This conceptual limitation led to *ignoring the store function* of money and, thus, made it impossible to perceive its financial issues.

This is obviously the second and, perhaps, most important point.

Regrettably, this subject is conspicuous by its absence from the history of ideas, and as far as can be observed, it has only been touched upon by Foucault.[35] However, it is most of all essential to note that Locke, on the other hand, fully mastered these functions, as the following passage, taken from a debate on lending, testifies:

> In Money there is a double Value, first as it is capable by its Interest to yield us such a yearly Income: in this it has the Nature of Land 2…as it is capable by Exchange to procure us the Necessaries…of Life…in this it has the Nature of a Commodity.
>
> (SC-49)

This is proof that as a philosopher, he had identified all the elements of this conceptual problem: from the criticism of metallism up to the idea of abstraction of money, the latter point having been noted by several recent commentators (Caffentzis,[36] Carey [2014], Garo[37] and Eich). This point will be dealt with in Chapter 5.

Nevertheless, these authors can be criticised for failing to identify that these issues were further intensified by another conceptual problem, this time related to the evaluation of values. But here again, this can be understood by returning to the comparison between the terms of a loan.

3.   A difficulty related to measurement by money.

Since in order to finalise this comparison, indeed, it was necessary to assess the paper and the coins, which means being able to measure them. But here again, these monetary movements failed, because such an evaluation could only be possible if it is carried out by a third party: which no movement was able to conceive at that time. To put it more precisely, they did not know *in what measure unit* values could be expressed, as the legal denomination (the unit of account) was unsuitable here because of the heterogeneity of species it referred to. This is the reason why these movements could not take into account the specificity of certain sensitive markets – such as 'bullion' (commercial metal) – which indeed raised the same difficulties. It should even be added that, for the same reasons, a 'value theory' of money could make no sense as some modern authors believed, in particular Appleby.[38]

In reality there was only one logical solution to these problems, which was to adopt a *specific norm*, compatible with these items, and which served as a way to measure the two supports that were being compared. For Locke this would be the *quantity of metal*.

But this was not easy to imagine, since giving money an additional attribute necessarily changed what *it was*. In other words, in order to think about this *function*, *the nature* of money had to be modified, which meant advocating a specific monetary policy that would guarantee it. Thus, inevitably leading to an *institutional* approach which can be summed up as:

> ==> An incompatibility between the physical conception of money and the measurement requirements related to credit. Below is Locke's position.

These were consequently *three problems which Locke's contemporary theories came up against, respectively: the function of credit, the 'store function' of money and the common measurement of its supports.* So, if this discussion makes sense, it is to show that they arose *specifically* in the debates that marked the creation of the Bank of England.

1.5 The thesis defended in this essay

The position defended in this essay can then be directly deduced in two points:

1. It was down to Locke to overcome these difficulties by proposing both a theoretical and practical vision of the monetary and financial issues at stake: practical meaning here that it was possible to provide an *operational* perspective to the decisions then at stake. This is how, fundamentally, Locke contributed to the institution of the Bank of England.
2. But, it is also that this theoretical answer was consistent with his own philosophy: which did not only imply a general *convergence* with his moral philosophy, but that it referred to the *very concepts* he developed. Now it is possible to resume with the example *of money* mentioned in the introduction and whose foundations in Natural Right had already been substantiated. Reiterating it:

> Mankind has made [of] gold and silver by general consent the common Pledges.
>
> (SC-31)

It is now easy to understand that this *philosophical* approach to money was in fact an answer to the measurement problem just mentioned. For Locke relied here on a specific theme – *convention* – which at the time was reputed to be linked to jusnaturalism. He was precisely referring to a *convention* on the status of pledge of metal – and *not of* money itself; and this affirmation amounts to arguing that metal served both as store value of money and this famous norm of measurement.[39]

That was the basis of his debate with Lowndes.

For beyond the fact that it was a credible solution to the theoretical problems that have just been mentioned, this standpoint was tantamount to deriving a theoretical concept – money – from moral principles: in this case, the justification of certain uses of money, whose stakes will be seen later on. The assumption defended here is that this approach was *systematic* for Locke, basing therefore his theoretical analysis on his philosophy.

1.5.1 The plan for this essay

From this point onwards, this essay's purpose becomes extremely straight-forward. Since it will amount only to *re-reading* the main texts of Locke to highlight these points that have just been discussed. This leads to the two main discussions below.

The first one is on the problems associated with the creation of the Bank of England and based on Locke's contribution to the parliamentary debate on interest. This contribution is recorded in his 'Considerations' where he explains the notion of function of banking and its regulation. Therefore, the following points will be seen:

- His *theory of interest* (Chapter 2) which, given its methodological importance, will be analysed independently;
- His *financial analysis* (Chapter 3) which includes the essence of his political standpoint on the role of banking, its link with savings and its regulation.

The second one is concerning the debates on the monetary reform, which reopened the question of the nature of money in relation to the topic of credit. This will be introduced through an excursus (Chapter 4) in order to re-problematise the debate on this subject. Then the following will be explained:

- Locke's *conception of money* (Chapter 5) which he would present as a political topic – hence national – and founded on a metal pledge, namely, its financial dimension. This point will be addressed from the main debates he led on this topic – with Lowndes and Pufendorf – and from his main economic writings.
- The *monetary policy* he advocated against Lowndes will be discussed at least from his 'Further Considerations' (Chapter 6). They will be read as a major contribution to the institutionalisation of a monetary and financial system – the real cutting edge of the financial revolution.

To conclude, there will be a discussion on the limits of Locke's commitment from the question of the Bank of England's status.

Such is the approach that will be adhered to and seen as consistent with the discussion conducted in this first chapter. The purpose is indeed to challenge Locke's economic philosophy in relation to the creation of the Bank of England.

However, there are consequences on the interpretation of Locke whether economic or philosophical. It would be better to say the problem raised by these interpretations. They have to be broached.

1.5.2 The anti-philosophical bias of Locke's interpretation

The first point concerns Locke's economic interpretation and it will be short, alas, since it is out of scope here. As was indicated at the outset, the problem with this interpretation is one of *method*. It is that the main economic historians have refused to consider the philosophical dimension of Locke's thinking and defending the independence of economic analysis.

This discussion, however, highlights the untenable character of such a standpoint.

Hence, the fact is that the vast majority of Locke's specialised readers have followed this approach, with very few exceptions, most of whom having already been cited, but to whom only Diatkine[40] or at a second level Berthoud[41] can be added. This can be appreciated from the following points: (1) this strange perspective, common to the majority of interpreters, and which led to read Locke by analogy with other economic movements – the interpretation being divided between two standpoints:

- The first one, already presented, judging Locke as a 'mercantilist', Blaug would say 'a later mercantislist'. Schumpeter is the most representative, but Hekscher [1955], Kelly, Carey, Horsefield and Dang.[42] De facto, Keynes can also be cited.
- The second one considering that Locke had anticipated liberal thinking by reasoning in terms of *economic laws*. Letwin, Vaughn,[43] Fay and de Boissieu will be cited, but the analysis of Vickers,[44] Fay, Appleby[45] and Marx will be challenged in Chapter 6. Here Letwin:

> Locke carried over into economics, the doctrine of natural law with its fusion of scientific principles and moral standards.[46]

Unfortunately, the distinctive characteristic of these movements was precisely their *positive* approach to the economy, and consequently their weakness on the points discussed here. This was, therefore, an insurmountable contradiction for Locke's interpretation.

(2) But undoubtedly, the most serious issue concerns the concept of *money*, the normative meaning of which could only be disregarded. This explains why Locke had almost systematically been credited with a *metallist* theory to which, however, he was explicitly opposed, as shall be seen (Chapter 2). Among a hundred examples, this one from Kelly:

> Locke showed himself to be apparently uncompromising metallist
> (Op. cit. p. 89)

It is a radical misinterpretation – even exceptional for such a discipline – because it referred to the structuring concept of any economic discourse. It is almost enough to explain the permanent gap that this interpretation will have with Locke's text.

However, the problem it raises for the consistency of this work should not go unheeded. It hinders this common approach to such research that relies on a consensus in interpretation and exceeds it only in certain aspects. This will not be possible here, and thus Locke's approach will need to be entirely reconstructed – to simply oppose it with the most common interpretations.

Therefore, the first approach should be just to re-read Locke's fundamental text: 'Some considerations on lowering interest …' in order to understand first and foremost *what the subject* was. This will be carried out with the following remark.

Concluding observation: money and the theory of property

While reaching the end of this chapter, it seems important to recall the extent of the debates that still take place today about Locke's philosophy, in particular, the surprising lack of consensus on some of his political views. This is the case with his well-known theory of property, which seems today to discourage the interpretation (Skinner). Yet, without claiming to be exhaustive, however, this debate about money should shed significant light on the matter.

It is indeed recognised that a major argument of this theory is focused on the theme of money (TCG-§45-51). It is Macpherson who called this to mind: for Locke it is money which authorises the 'extension' of ownership. However, it has hardly been noted that Locke's approach to advancing this theme was similar to the one just read in his 'Considerations': through a convention on metal only. He spoke precisely of a 'consent' on its value and only on the use of money:

> Agreement…more than real use…has put the value on Gold and Silver
>
> (TCG-§46)

The question to be asked, therefore, is the reason for this similarity for it invalidates current interpretations, which are almost always based on a confusion between 'metal' and 'money' (see Chapter 5 for further details).

It is obviously a complex question, which refers to the *moral status* of this theory, that is to say, its connection with the *State of Nature*. It seems, however, possible to respond provided that we recognise that its context was a debate *within the jusnaturalism*, described in detail by Tully[47] regarding its juridical dimension. But this debate went even further – notably with Pufendorf – to include questions of money and the status of its use.

The author's position is then that the role of this assertion was to go beyond the historical position of Natural Right – known as 'prohibitionist' – which rejected the use of money as a *store of value*. It was in fact the standpoint of Aquinus who had defined money as a *conventional measuring instrument*: a theme that Locke and Pufendorf would take up with them. However, he did so in such a restrictive way that metal was for him neutralised in the act of measurement – so it had no economic value – which prohibited any idea of 'value storing' and the uses linked to it – hence the theme of a money which 'prohibited' interest:

> [For Aquinus] moneyed-metal used for exchange is destroyed by use…like the wine we drink.[48]

This is why this work states that the primary purpose of this metal convention was to lift this restriction, even if this point is still badly identified. The proof of this is the argument following immediately this definition – the so-called 'nut argument' – which clearly substantiates this idea of store of value (see also Diatkine on this point):

> Thus came in the use of money, some lasting thing that man might keep…and that by mutual consent men would take in exchange… for…supports of life.
>
> (TCG-§47)

It should be commented on as follows: (1) Locke does not justify, as has been sustained, an *accumulation* function that would be specific to money – Caffentzis,[49] Théret [2014]. Because the explicit reference here is the *pledge* which always restores the value within time (what Locke means by the term 'exchange'). (2) On the other hand, he justifies the notion of 'store of value', since money is here a 'lasting' object, which could be reinvested afterwards in order to expand property (TCG-§48). It must therefore be concluded that the purpose of this argument was to justify the uses linked to this function of storage: the theory of property being based on savings, and Locke's economic writings focusing on lending (predominantly). This is why the hypothesis formulated – and subject to certain limits yet to be specified – is:

> ==> that Locke's theory of property had this function of justifying a market dynamic regarding land but based on saving.

This is quite clearly merely a hypothesis, since this discussion has just touched on the *beginning* of Locke's argument. In particular, its methodological issues, which refer to its moral status, and namely the idea of general interest, have been ignored. This calls, therefore, for a more in-depth analysis. However, it already proves that it is possible to reconstruct the meaning of Locke's treatise from his economic opinions.

This is what will be gradually carried out here at the end of each of the chapters of this book in order to preserve the independent nature of this discussion. Nonetheless, this makes it all the more necessary to have a closer look at Locke's economic opinions, and in particular, those recorded in his 'Some Considerations'.

It is regrettable that it is not more highly considered today, because this work has a story that is meant to attract attention. Initiated as early as the 1670s, it is considered to have closed the long theoretical debate on interest that went on throughout the 17th century. But above all, it was rewritten in 1691 in anticipation of the famous Parliamentary debate which could be argued as having started the financial revolution. Therefore, this text – in a rather native way, so to speak – included both the theoretical and political dimensions of this revolution.

Even after all these years, they have still not received the interpretation they deserved.

Notes

1 '*The theory of possessive individualism*', 1990.
2 GDP and State expenses are, respectively, estimated at £41 million (m) and £3.5m in 1688 (North), and £47m and £7.9m in 1697 (Davenant). Unspecified data from Mitchell [1962].
3 In Clapham, '*History of the bank*'.
4 North-Weingast, '*Constitutions and commitment*', 1989.
5 '*A brief account of the intended Bank of England*', 1693, p. 4. This situation was due, in particular, to the crisis of 1675 when the State declared itself insolvent.
6 For these points, see Horsefield (Op. cit.).
7 This model actually created the illusion of a collective guarantee of the notes that were issued, but without insuring the cash equivalent. It was abandoned after several failures, including Law's in 1720, and Locke was very hostile to

it. It has, however, been highlighted by several recent commentators who saw it as the beginning of modern banking practices (namely, Wennerlind).

8 In Dickson, '*The financial revolution*', 1967, p. 12.

9 Several recent authors have made this criticism to Locke and, namely, Carey who concluded that '*Locke was doubtful about the role of credit*', which is not acceptable: it is hard to see why Locke would have invested so much in conceiving theory about it (in '*The empire of credit*', 2007, p. 26).

10 '*Thy resolved to run counter to all Mankind...cried down the use of gold...and up that of other materials*' (Paterson Op. cit., p. 3).

11 '*Angliae tutamen*' through Dickson Op. cit., p. 15. See also Godfrey [1888].

12 This expression, even though from the 19th century, is probably the best one.

13 Letter to Clarke and Freke 18/02/1695. In De Beer, *The correspondence of Locke*, 1979.

14 In '*The nine first years of the Bank of England.*', 2001, p. 9.

15 This is what Paterson implies when he explains that the shareholders will not take dividends on the income from the loan to the state: '*thus a society of private men will be obliged ... to strengthen ... the public security of this Bank*', (Op. cit., p. 11).

16 '*[as opposed to] Appleby...I believe that Locke had his eyes... on the new system of credit*', Op.cit., pp. 135.

17 In '*Whence and Whither Money*'? (2002).

18 This will be done (every 4/5) by redeeming 'tallies', a practice that would become a rule, and which would, to a certain extent, seal the interdependence of the Bank and the State (Dickson). See also Chapter 6.

19 See particularly his letter dated 6/8/1694 where he encouraged Clarke to stay at the head of the Bank '*with no small consequence for England*' (De Beer-Op. cit). Clarke was his main political leverage.

20 According to Kelly, Op.cit., p. 103.

21 Adhesion to Schumpeter, who distinguishes between two forms of 'mercantilism': in a doctrinal sense, the term refers to the well-known trade policy; in a theoretical sense, it refers to the mode of conceptualisation discussed here. He will be followed by Foucault.

22 Mun, '*a discorse of trade*', 1621, p. 59.

23 See in particular his '*History*', Op cit, pp. 283–284, pp. 288–294, pp. 327–331.

24 Hegeland in '*The theory quantitative theory of money*', 1988, p. 26.

25 'Mercantilism' was a 'metallism' that confused, in addition, capital and money. The notion lost its usefulness in judging monetary debates.

26 '*A new discorse of trade*', 1698, p. XXVI.

27 Culpeper, '*Treatise against usury*', From the French Translation (FFT)-1754; North, '*Discourses upon trade*', *1691*.

28 In '*Treatise on taxes*', FFT-1906, p. 42. Petty defended this original view deriving the value of money from its cost of production, but basically he remained a metallist.

29 '*Two manuscripts concerning ... coin ... and credit*', 1942, p. 20; Cary, '*An essay on the coin*', 1696.

30 Vaughan, '*A treatise of money*', 1675; Barbon, '*A discorse concerning coining...*', 1696 – *An essay on the coin*, 1696, p. 5.

31 '*Report concerning...the amendment of sliver coins*', 1695; Hodges, '*The present state of England*', 1697; Temple, '*Short remarks about M Lock's book*', 1696.

32 Schumpeter defines cartalism as '*the exact opposite of metallism*'. This discussion shows that this is not exact.

33 The theory distinguishes between the idea of *store value* where money retains value but for restoring it (the pledge paradigm), and *accumulation*, which it rejects because it would make money a capital that is hoarded. The distinction is essential here because Locke will retain the first idea and denounce 'hoarding' (Chapters 3 and 6).

34 Vaughan will have the opposite attitude, as will be seen better in Locke's critique (Chapter 2).

35 Foucault showed precisely the inability of mercantilism to attain the idea of abstraction: 'money...is the...instrument of representation of wealth... in which there is no longer any intermediary figure to connect the sign to the signified', '*The order of things*', 2002, pp. 70,190.

36 The most stimulating of these is Caffentzis to whom we owe the rehabilitation of the philosophical and institutional dimension of money at Locke. But without understanding its financial dimension, this will be shown in the following pages: in '*clipped coins, abused words and civil government...*', 1989.

37 '*Monnaie et richesse*', 2000; Eich, '*Locke and the politics...of depolitization*', 2018.

38 It is through such 'theories of value' that modern theory overcomes this measurement difficulty. But the point is that these theories were *inaccessible* at that time because they still presuppose a homogeneity of money that did not yet exist. It is therefore by mistake that Appleby attributes their first formalisation to Locke's contemporaries (cf. Chapter 6).

39 '*Silver is the measure of commerce by its quantity*', (FC-2).

40 Diatkine is credited with highlighting the financial dimension of Locke's thinking: 'Locke definit la monnaie comme une "réserve de valeur"', in '*De la convention...*', 1986. But while confusing metal with money, he failed to understand its finality: this will be seen in Chapter 2 about the notion of 'double value'.

41 One of the few economists to recognise the jusnaturalist character of Locke's money, but without developing it. In '*morale et enrichissement*', 1988 (see also Böhm-Bawerk-[1902]).

42 '*Monnaie, libéralisme et cohésion sociale*', 1997.

43 '*Locke as an economist and a social scientist*', 1980.

44 '*Studies in the theory of money*', 1960; Fay, '*Locke versus Lowndes*', 1933.

45 For Appleby see also '*Economic thought and ideology in the 17th century*', 1978; for Marx see Chapters 5 and 6.

46 In '*The origins of scientifical economics*', 1983, p. 176.

47 In '*a discourse on property*', 1980, pp. 77–94.

48 Van Roey, '*La monnaie d'après St Thomas...*', 1905, p. 217.

49 '*Invention of money created a...polarity between accumulation and scarcity...the rich and depossessed*', (Op. cit.). In Chapter 5, the consequences of this error will be discussed. Théret supported this standpoint.

2 The theory of interest and the Natural Right

The main body of Locke's economic viewpoint is contained in his first text '*Some considerations upon lowering interest…*', which deals with ways of overcoming the financial crisis that England was experiencing. In fact, this text is a rewriting of old working notes, known as '*Early writings*', which Locke turned into an address to Parliament to challenge the proposed lowering of interest by law: '*I think, generally speaking… 'tis manifest it cannot*' declares the opening sentence of the 'Considerations'. The allusion was clear, and would be perceived by all commentators.

But that would be the only point to be understood.

Yet the 'Considerations' were not just confined to criticising this law. Otherwise, they would have been inaudible. Their purpose was to counter it with an alternative financial policy, which would be outlined in astonishingly modern terms as *regulation of the banking system*. As a basis for this proposal, Locke would put forward an essential argument but one that would require substantiation: the inescapable, but also monopolistic, character of banking intermediation.

This was very clearly stated at the outset, from the first two assertions in the 'Considerations', which should be considered as a summary of his standpoint. The first assertion was even extremely precise, since it explained that the law could not prevent this intermediation role; it also means that this was far from being accepted at that time:

> You cannot hinder Men, skill'd in the Power they have over their own Goods, and the ways of Conveying them to others, to purchase Money to be Lent them <u>at what Rate soever their Occasions shall make it necessary</u> for them to have it.
>
> (SC-1,2; all underlined passages are our own)

The second assertion is discussed below. The conclusion will then be unequivocal:

[B]ut when a kind of Monopoly - [banks] - by consent, has put this general Commodity into a few Hands, it may need regulation.

(SC–103,104)

The 'Considerations' were, therefore, a *finalised* text and clearly defined by what could be called the '*banking question*' and its necessary regulation. Here it is argued that this text heralded the financial revolution.

2.1 The issue of understanding the 'Considerations'

Unfortunately, and despite the obviousness of these passages, this conclusion remains misunderstood by the interpretation, and to such an extent that there is still silence about it. Thus, among the observers, only one of them accurately mentioned this theme of regulation – Tucker;[1] but no comment from either Marx or Schumpeter, nor even Keynes who was however favourable to Locke.[2] On the contrary, many would credit him with an opposite view, that of the liberalisation of the financial system (Letwin, Vaughn and so on). Finally, there was regrettably an obvious error in the scientific edition of the 'Considerations'.[3]

Such blindness seems to be without precedent in the history of economic thought, which has traditionally focused on in-depth research on the authors. It first and foremost explains the silence surrounding the financial revolution. But without trying to apologise, an explanation can be formulated from the theoretical dimension of Locke's texts and the method he used. The specificity of the 'Considerations' is that they approached these issues from a *normative* perspective and in order to distinguish what would be a monopolistic practice and a legitimate one in the financial world.

It is first of all this point that remains unidentified.

2.1.1 The normative perspective of the 'Considerations'

It is clear, however, from this second argument where Locke refers to the monopolistic nature of banks. In this argument, indeed, Locke raises the hypothesis of a fall in interest to emphasise the gap that would appear between the rates paid to savers and those paid by entrepreneurs: this gap being indicative of a monopolistic practice. But, he would do so on the basis of a norm – called *natural interest* – which would enable this gap to be evaluated: his argument being that the bankers knew this norm and how to subvert the law to their advantage (Locke almost described this as a form of 'carry trade'):

It will...increase the Advantage of Bankers and scriveners...Who skilled in the Arts of putting out Money according to the true and natural Value, which the present State of Trade, Money and Debts, shall always raise Interest to, they will infallibly get, what the true Value of Interest shall be, above the Legal.

(SC-2,3)

It was then in relation to this norm that he would build his theoretical system, and in particular, the theory of interest which is at the core: by stressing both its roots in the real economy, and the need to use it as a base for 'bank regulation'. The law, he said, must ultimately be linked to it.

Hence, it is the use of this norm that the interpretation failed to identify. Almost all commentators have adopted the strange attitude of reading the 'Considerations' only through a positive lens – this norm being assimilated to a simple fact – which inevitably detracted from its meaning. This is the case with Letwin and authors who followed him, who credited Locke with a 'law' on interest, here in the sense of scientific law, even claiming that it would have led him to refuse any political initiative:

[E]conomic affairs [were]...misgoverned by any positive law, that do not accord with natural law.

(Op. cit., p. 176)

There cannot be greater opposition to Locke's standpoint.

But it is also the case of Schumpeter, and the authors who followed him, who credited Locke with the fact that he reasoned entirely from a mercantilist perspective which means here from a pure market perspective. This is why he would qualify his theory of interest as 'monetary theory', and he would describe it as the representation of a financial arbitrage:

[H]is may be...an embryonic form of...the Swedish...theory: interest is explained by a demand proceeding from expected profits and meeting a supply of 'loanable funds'.

(Op. cit., p. 329)

It is this kind of analysis that is challenged here, despite Schumpeter's authority; and for two reasons.

1. Firstly, by attributing to him a 'monetary' reasoning, Locke was denied any coherent financial analysis, and furthermore, any idea

of financial regulation. More precisely, he was denied any idea of a link between the real economy and interest, which is essential for such an analysis. Chapter 1 explained the reason. But that is exactly this link that can be read from Locke's just cited quotations, and the underlined passages clearly indicate this. The term *realism* can be deployed here. It can therefore be stated from now on that Locke did not deal with interest as Schumpeter maintained, which to the author's knowledge only Tucker has noted,[4] and partially Leigh.[5] It can even be presumed that by neglecting such a point, Schumpeter overlooked the very core of Locke's theoretical system and even the principles of his regulatory project.

==> Thus, the initial aim here will be to reconstruct the meaning of this system in order to understand how it contributed to the theme of regulation.

2.1.2 The philosophical origins of Locke's economic theory

2. However, if this thesis is to be contested, it is also for a reason of method and this is a direct reference to the philosophy. Indeed, his 'mercantilism' that was attributed to Locke was already a structured way of thinking. It was even formed against the previous widespread normative approach, in particular that of Natural Right (Letwin[6]). If it is true, therefore, that Locke picked up on this again, he could not do so without a fundamental debate with such a movement, but this discussion was also missed. The proof of this is the controversial argument that Locke planted at the heart of his theory, which was aimed at the well-known fetishism of the 'mercantilists' and their confusion between money and capital. The formula was very widely known at that time (Böhm-Bawerk):

Money is a barren thing and produces nothing.

(SC-55)

As Locke took that over, it means that he knew both the 'mercantilist' weaknesses but also that he was trying to overcome them – which already contradicts several important interpretations.[7] Yet, as is now known, such a debate necessarily involved philosophy, and this can only mean one thing: that Locke dealt with these points from the point of view of Natural Right. And it is argued here that it is this philosophical approach that gave his financial analysis its political meaning. This is a far cry from Schumpeter.

==> So, the second purpose of this discussion will be to clarify this point.

But if this analysis is right, it requires a specific approach and to give critical importance to the theoretical dimension of the 'Considerations'. Admittedly, this is a very technical area for the discussion being carried out here. Its first result, however, suggests that Locke's efforts were essentially focused on this aspect, and that it contained his main funding ideas. This will be demonstrated as follows by dividing 'Some considerations' into two parts:

- The theory of interest that forms the basis of Locke's economic thinking – Chapter 2. It will be highlighted through the following points:
  - That Locke put forward a *realistic* theory of interest, as defined above. It will be described through an analogy with the Keynesian one,
  - That he did so in *normative* terms, which led to the idea of an economic function for credit which would be the basis of his financial analysis,
  - And, on all these points through a *philosophical debate* with the mercantilist tradition.
- The resulting political and financial analysis, which would lead Locke to the topic of financial regulation – Chapter 3. Subsequently, the following points will be addressed:
  - That Locke developed there the concept of a financial *function,*
  - Which was supported *by savings,*
  - And that he would lay here the foundations of his theme *of regulation.*

It is consequently through the interpretation of Locke's theory of interest that this work should now proceed. However, this discussion would lose some of its meaning if it were not placed historically, and particularly in relation to mercantilist thinking. For Locke's theory was based on the criticism of those ideas. That is, therefore, the appropriate starting point.

2.2 Locke's normative meaning of natural interest

Indeed, it is difficult to approach Locke's theory of interest without thinking about it in relation to the ideas of his time, and in particular, to the long debate on interest that marked the 17th century. This debate is widely known because it attracted the best economists of the time. It is often described as the achievement of a still budding theory that set out to imagine financial mechanisms. However, this effort was often considered to be unsuccessful (Letwin).

On the one hand, these authors are considered to have been able to point out some of the causes of underfinancing, by emphasising the link between money in circulation and trade balance (Mun, Misselden[8]) or interest rates. Over a long period of time, many of Locke's contemporaries would have taken these points for granted. But on the other hand, these authors stumbled over this macroeconomic problem that has been identified: the relationship that must be traced between interest rate and the productive economy. Schumpeter would speak of the 'profit rate'.

This issue, as is known, had a conceptual origin. It stemmed from the fact that almost all these authors addressed interest in monetary terms, that is, as a price in a market. This was the case, as was observed with Mun, but also with North. The main point of this view, however, is to be found elsewhere: that as a consequence of this market approach, financial issues could only be discussed in terms of *arbitrage*, in other words, by only pointing out the way key participants could adapt to this 'market price'. The example of both Culpepers can be cited, here the father:

> As soon as our traders have acquired a sizeable fortune, they give up trading and prefer to lend their money.
>
> (Op. cit. p. 442)

What should be understood, however, is that interest could just as well be considered as an *administrable price*, because in fact nothing changed in the reasoning. This happened frequently, like with Manley[9] who is sometimes compared to Locke. It would moreover be the case for Child, who was at that time the leading economist, and who would make low interest the focus of all his propositions:

> The profit that people received by reducing the interest...in my opinion is the causa causans of the riches.
>
> (Op. cit. p. 8)

It would be wrong to disregard the significance of this view.

Yet this was an illusion, because by doing so, Child was unaware that interest was already highly dependent on the profitability of companies – which is a *realistic dependence* – and of the consequences of this. He focussed only on the immediate effects of a low interest.

This point needs to be acknowledged while reading Locke.

2.2.1 The notion of natural interest

Since what made the 'Considerations' so specific is that they dealt with interest from an idea that was unheard of, but which would be defined by this link with the real economy: *natural interest*. So, in the previous quotation, Locke spoke of the level at which '*Trade, Money and Debts shall raise interest*', which is a realistic presentation of interest. On condition, however, adding that this natural rate did not replace what is called 'the' interest rate, in other words, the effective and/or legal rate. In fact, Locke also accepted both notions, because his aim was to understand their relationship, or namely, their divergence; and this duality should be seen as the starting point for his analysis.

This was expressed very clearly, moreover, in this famous second argument, already quoted, but just as much in the commentary below:

> [S]o that the rate you set, profits not the lenders, and very few of the borrowers, who...pay the price for money, that commodity would bear.

(SC-6)

Indeed, there was a similar approach in both quotations. Firstly, the gap that appears between the two rates – natural and effective – was highlighted. However, it needed to be interpreted, and it would be through the *relationship* between the natural rate and the borrower's activity ('he pays the price' says Locke). But in doing so, this also provided an opportunity to judge the banker's activity and affirm this gap as a sign of dysfunctions. This was carried out, above all, from a global perspective, because these dysfunctions were judged from the perspective of the real economy; and this already traced what the *function* of credit would be. It can therefore be assumed that the 'Considerations' did indeed propose a realistic theory of interest, which could attain the idea of a *function* for credit.

However, in order to assess this, the *type* of innovation that Locke introduced with this natural interest must be examined, including its critical scope with regard to the 'mercantilist' theories.

As mentioned at the outset, these theories were formed in opposition to an erstwhile approach, inspired by Natural Right, which denounced lending with interest. From that point on, speaking of natural interest had a double meaning. Firstly, it meant that Locke assumed the critical stance of the mercantilists with regard to his own tradition; he would call his supporters 'over-scrupulous men'.[10] But, it also meant that he took the approach of Natural Right in his own name – to apply it to interest – but against mercantilism. This approach was still known at that time, and the best is here to refer to Schumpeter who described it as the assertion of norms, corresponding to fair competitive conditions but which could be interpreted as 'values obtained under optimal competitive conditions' – see hereafter Schumpeter's argument.[11]

This was, moreover, close to Locke's definition.

On this basis, the fact that there was a *natural* interest suggested, for Locke, that it was a norm of value for financial loans and that this norm was the result of general economic conditions. This can be called therefore a 'normative realism'.

2.2.2 The 'Considerations' analysis method

However, it is too early to conclude on that. For it could be objected that it was the *natural interest* as such that was the subject of a monetary analysis – in other words, that it could be described through the supply and demand for loans. This is how Kelly would understand it, clarifying in fact Schumpeter's theory:

> Locke sets out to show that interest as the price of the hire of money…determined by the number of buyers and sellers.
>
> (Op. cit. p. 72)

However, it was also Dang's thesis, which spoke of an abstract norm concerning the natural rate.[12] Vaughn in another way credited Locke with a 'law of interest formation', as did also Macaulay.[13]

Actually, that would not make much sense, because it is hard to see, among these authors, why Locke would exclude the world of banking from the formation of natural interest. However, this facilitates the understanding of how Locke thought out the *role* of this natural rate, and furthermore, how he determined effective interest. For what Kelly missed, together with many other readers, are the methodological consequences of this *idea* of natural interest, that is, the consequences of raising such a hypothesis; and above all, the fact that they would be incompatible with the monetary analysis.

For admittedly, it could be assumed that this natural rate was a result, the only result of economic activity. However, it was still necessary to describe how it influenced banking behaviour, and this inevitably led to a distinction between *two levels* of reasoning, at least one of which was normative: the first level would correspond to the real setting of this rate, and would transcribe a practice, while the second level would describe the corresponding behavioural adaptations, this rate then becoming as a *binding* reality. This was tantamount to setting a norm.

Now it is this coherence – these two levels – which can be understood from the 'Considerations', respectively:

1. A short-term plan that covers what is called the financial world, and describes how effective interest and its spread with the natural rate were formed.

It was, for instance, in this plan that Locke explained his position on the phenomenon of *carry trade*. Then, logically also, he used this plan to defend his argument in favour of banking regulation. It is interesting to underline that he would anticipate this position with a critique of monetary analysis, which was inappropriate for a bank-oriented world:

> If Money were to be hired…from the Owner himself…it might… probably be had at the Market…Rate, But [not] when a kind of Monopoly…has put [money] into a few Hands….
>
> (SC-103)

These analyses then make up the core of his political message, respectively, in the first and last part of the 'Considerations'. These will only be covered, however, in a second stage – Chapter 3.

2. For Locke inevitably had to anticipate this debate through a more in-depth theoretical analysis, which would enable him to determine this natural rate. That was precisely what he would do in a second phase, *focusing on the long term*, and logically more complex (SC, pp. 44–72). For it would embody all the elements of what is called 'the real economy' in order to attain this natural rate. This will be described hereafter.

The similarity with the Keynesian IS/LM model is obvious here.

What Locke's interpreters failed to understand, then, is this latter point: that this *dual* approach to interest was necessarily in conflict with a monetary analysis, and this was so because of an unquestionable separation between the characteristics relating (1) to the supply and demand for loans – which here were short term, and (2) the determinants of natural interest. In fact, *this only made sense* in a Natural Right approach.

2.2.3 Locke's critique of mercantilism

However, this mistake was more serious than that because by associating Locke's position with the mercantilists, any criticism was evaded on purpose as he wilfully contested their standpoints. This debate was unavoidable, however, since they were the predominant school of thought. On this basis, this section on determining the natural rate should also be read at two levels:

- A *positive* level where Locke would actually determine this natural rate, which implied calculating it,
- But a calculation based on a *critique* of the mercantilist position, so that he could put forward his own ideas.
- It is, therefore, quite regrettable that this aspect of the 'Considerations' is so inadequately interpreted today. Thus, as previously observed, the weaknesses of mercantilist thinking affected major topics, but which could only be overcome with the help of philosophy. It should therefore be acknowledged that this was a crucial juncture where Locke had to mobilise his own philosophical principles in order to merely set out theoretical concepts, in other words, to lay down their philosophical foundations.

Such an event is extremely rare in economics, and that is why the simplest way to measure it is to follow the step-by-step arguments by which Locke would determine natural interest.

Two distinct movements can be discerned: the critical then quantitative determination of the natural interest rate.

2.3 Critical determination of natural interest

This critical determination is the most significant theoretical passage in the 'Considerations', because Locke would base the idea of the natural interest on it. It consists of *four phases.*

1. Firstly, a moment of *pure criticism,* where Locke would *contest* the mercantilist perception of money from its epistemological confines (SC, pp. 44–49).

As observed in Chapter 1, the real weakness of these authors was their incapacity to represent the notion of 'value of money', because they did not know how to distinguish between these two notions of its intermediation value and its store value. This was due – as has been explained – to their material vision of money which they shared with the other monetary schools of thought. Locke would therefore take an emblematic example of this dilemma, referring to a formulation that was prominent at the time and to which he credited *'a man of no small influence'* – probably Vaughan.[14]

That the lowering of Interest will raise the value of all other Things in proportion.

(SC-44)

He then refuted it – at length – arguing that a change in the interest rate did not alter the intermediation function of money, at least in the short term, which is difficult to contest:

The fall therefore or rise of Interest...alters not at all the Value of Money, in reference to Commodities.

(SC-48,49)

However, the real meaning of this argument was a logical one. It was first that this mistake was made not for empirical reasons, but because the two values of money could not be represented *simultaneously* – this criticism being valid for the whole of mercantilism.[15] In doing so, however, he gave himself the means of his own conception which coincides, as is now known, with the modern vision of functions.

2. This was then a founding time, because Locke set down this idea basing himself on a thesis unheard of at the time, but which is well known through modern theory: that money had several values, several meaning that they could be assigned a particular use, while *coexisting* at a theoretical level.

This is cited again below; it describes what we call 'monetary functions':

In Money there is a double Value, first as it is capable by its Interest to yield us...a yearly income...2...as it is capable by Exchange to procure...the Necessaries...of Life.

(SC-49)

Such a quotation, dare it be said, is historical. For it must be underlined that these monetary functions form the very precondition of macroeconomics; and this was the first time that the idea appeared in the literature. It should, therefore, be recognised as the first positive step in this discipline.[16] It is indeed unfortunate that none of Locke's readers was able to pinpoint this innovation.

However, this calls for an additional observation, which refers to the underlying definition of money. Since as has most probably been noted, only the *epistemological* part of Locke's positions has been presented here, omitting to mention the question of the *nature* of money, even though it is addressed well before this passage (SC, pp. 31–33). This is not, however, a mistake made on purpose here, but a choice of layout that leaves this question for the final part of this work. This choice is justified, however, by the fact that this notion of monetary functions is sufficient logical so as to follow Locke's conception of interest.

3. For this reason, and at the same time as he was asserting this *'dual value'*, Locke would focus on redefining credit *at a theoretical level*. He would do so, once again, in a controversial way (SC, pp. 54–55).

Because at that time – and this has been explained at length – credit was thought of only in terms of exchange, whereas it was *a contract*, which was much more complex to conceptualise. It was therefore essential to redefine it in order to put forward a coherent theory. That is precisely what Locke would do, in what was then the essential passage in this discussion, and Macpherson has to be supported on this point.[17] '*Money is a barren thing and produces nothing*', says Locke, it is now known:

> [B]ut by Compact transfers that Profit that was the Reward of one Man's Labour into another Man's Pocket.
>
> (SC-55)

The statement is clear, and it can be understood that it closed the discussion with mercantilists. It actually means that Locke had to make a philosophical detour to arrive at his own views on credit. However, the crucial point was to be able to produce a theory that could represent credit in both dimensions: loan and interest.

4. This was precisely what Locke was going to do, *during the calculation phase*, by choosing to rely on the model of tenant farming, whose pedagogical interest was obvious at the time (SC, pp. 55–57).

It was in fact an omnipresent model at that time and its contractual nature was widely acknowledged. Furthermore, it had the advantage of revealing a clear and realistic link, in the sense of this discussion, between the value of the rent and the farmer's activity. It was thus possible to use this model as a basis *for an analogy* for this famous theory of interest.

The whole argument can be cited here, because the key message is in the way it is formulated:

> [T]he unequal Distribution of Money has the same effect...upon Land, that it has upon Money...For as the unequal Distribution

of Land...brings you a Tenant for your Land...the same unequal Distribution of Money... brings me a Tenant for my Money... [and he pays] use...For the same Reason...the Tenant pays Rent for your Land.

(SC-55,56)

It is easy to see that this passage is arranged into two sub-arguments that are sufficient for this determination. Locke did indeed explain here then:

1. That interest required a loan in money, where the terms were a matter of supply and demand. This is what he meant by the expression '*inequality of land...*', the meaning of which being also that there was a market for land, as will be seen better hereafter.

This suggests that Locke saw money supply as a determinant of the interest rate, which was widely accepted at the time. The determinants of this supply will be discussed in the next chapter.

2. But, the interest itself would be determined specifically and, above all, *outside* of this interaction between supply and demand. Consequently, the fact of representing interest as a contract made it possible to present it as a *sharing of income* resulting from a rational calculation.

Locke would then be crystal clear on the rules of this sharing, explaining, again by this analogy, that they related *only to the borrower's income*, originating from the investment. The following expression can be cited – which underpins this idea of sharing – because the important point here is to acknowledge its realistic character:[18]

So his Six per Cent. may seem to be the Fruit of another Man's Labour, yet he shares not...much of the profit of another Man's Labour, as he that lets Land to a Tenant.

(SC-56)

The conclusion is now inevitable. So, it is manifest that according to Locke, the borrower's income was the second force determining natural interest. In other words, and bringing the two proposals together, Locke would argue that natural interest *was at the confluence of two quantitative logics*: the change in supply and corporate profitability – each one acting in an intuitive way. It would therefore be concluded that this was a realistic position and that this type of calculation did make it possible to determine interest.

This was indeed a coherent reasoning, which not only acknowledged the aporias of 'mercantilist' thinking, but also satisfied the requirements of a credit theory.

> ==> It is therefore not true that Locke proposed a monetary analysis of interest; on the contrary, he put forward a realistic analysis that was consistent with the financial issues involved. Such will be the main result of this chapter.

This is, however, only a partial result and it is worth evaluating the reason. As the question being asked in this chapter is primarily one of method. It is whether Locke did everything possible to carry out normative and coherent financial analysis, and this has been proven. Therefore, any further discussion could be curtailed here in order to focus on the financial counterparties.

2.4 Quantitative determination of natural interest

It is thought-provoking to pursue Locke's demonstration up until the complete – quantified – determination of this natural interest. Because it can be qualified as a historical moment, that of the birth of macroeconomic theory – following Keynes anyway. It therefore had to face some of the difficulties that economic theory would subsequently encounter – particularly regarding the question of value. There were, above all, too many misunderstandings about it to leave room for ambiguity.

It will be easier, however, to follow Locke's thinking. Hence, having put forward a calculation model for interest, all he had to do was to deploy it to accomplish a complete theory. In the end, this only confronted him with epistemological difficulties.

2.4.1 Calculation method requirements

1. He first had to complete its interest calculation in the case of a personal loan, which required clarification of the rules governing the sharing of income between the different partners.

He would do so on the assumption of a fair distribution between lender and borrower. It was, however, a fairly simple idea that was not his own, but also in Culpeper. However, in this case, it referred to these complex notions of *marginal income* and even *marginal efficiency of capital* (the extra income obtained from an investment financed by a loan is called 'marginal income'). These were genuine conceptual innovations – which Keynes would pick up on again – and required a sophisticated mastery of differential calculus. It is asserted here that Locke carried them out:

> [M]y Money is apt in Trade, by the Industry of the Borrower, to produce more than 6% to the Borrower, as well as Land, by the Labour of the Tenant, is apt to produce more Fruits, than his Rent comes to.
>
> (SC-56)

Above all, however, this passage should be read as a key step in Locke's reasoning:

2. Because this famous natural interest rate was obtained by generalising this calculation, generalising meaning here: also to incorporate in the same reasoning all the loan contracts at a given period.

There was then, nevertheless, a final difficulty, which several commentators have also encountered, and this deserves an explanation. This is because in making such a calculation, Locke was necessarily referring to different activities whose profitability logic had to converge towards the same rate (wheat and barley, for example). It was therefore necessary to be able to *compare* the income from these activities, at least intellectually. But this was only possible with *a price theory* providing here the income – and therefore a *value theory* that would provide the basis for this comparison.

That is what Locke did.

However, it should be noted that this value-based approach was already known at that time. Petty, for example – even if his approach was specific[19] – mastered it in a sufficient epistemological way, and Locke was well aware of it. On the other hand, this question presented itself in a completely new light for him because of his reference to money. As it should be remembered that, at the time, these calculations were approached from a *material* vision of money that allowed such an equivalence. This was also the case with Petty. But Locke rejected this vision. That is why, and again in a logical way, it became essential for him to base his calculation on a complete revaluation of market theory, which incorporated his own vision of money.

This explains why Locke inserted a long theoretical parenthesis, where he would attempt to re-evaluate these notions, but starting from the idea of a monetary function – in this case an intermediation function (SC, pp. 62–69). An answer to Foucault is presented hereafter.[20]

2.4.2 Analysis of the market phenomenon

This can, however, be quite short. For in reality, it was only a question of re-obtaining known elements, but from the 'intermediation function' of money. So it was only a question of logic, and Locke was a master at that. Thus, it will simply be noted that he fully assumed this problem, broaching, respectively:

1. The concept of exchange value, through the expression hereafter, equating it to an inventory turnover rate. It can be supposed that Locke borrowed this definition from the trading community:

> He that will…estimate the value of anything must consider its quantity in relation to the vent.[21]

(SC-61)

2. The notion of market price and its corollary, income. Locke correctly stated:

> Value determine[s] the price of commodities.

(SC-61)

3. And, that of the *value of money* – read here: in its intermediation function – which was in fact, but with more than a slight difference,[22] the first expression of the well-known quantitative theory of money (QTM):

> This being so, its quantity alone is enough to regulate and determine its value, without considering any Proportion between its quantity and vent.

(SC-71)

These points have been mentioned by many commentators and need not be elaborated upon. However, the lack of rigour in the comments is to be regretted: on the one hand, because very few would underline the epistemological dimension of Locke's approach, but above all, for the genuine misinterpretations that have been made.

It is, therefore, important to specify that this was by no means a labour-value theory, as Marx believed,[23] and even less a general theory of value (Vaughn,[24] Diatkine).

4. The proof of this is that Locke would close this discussion with a specific debate on the price of capital, whose difference with value must be underlined – in this case it is the 'supply price' of capital (Keynes) and its *present value* (as theorised by Petty). He would do so at great length,

since this value was often used to call for a drop in interest.[25] He would then demonstrate the empirical unrealism of this position basing himself on historical facts (SC-58), and then reveal that capital gave rise to a market phenomenon.

> All Things…raise and fall their price…as there are more Buyers or Sellers. This Rule holds in Land as well as all other Commodities.
>
> (SC-59,60)

But by also stipulating that the request was specific here because it was essentially dependent on savings. Keynes, moreover, borrowed this idea. There is, therefore, only a theory of price and not of value. (These aspects will be covered from the perspective of savings in Chapter 3.)

If this approach is accepted, then it is possible to accept that natural interest can be calculated, since it was sufficient to relate this market price theory to his previous result on the efficiency of capital.

2.4.3 Towards Locke's financial analysis: the calculation of natural interest

This was what Locke did in the section immediately following this passage (SC, pp. 69–72). In fact, it would be a simple generalisation of the previous calculation, concluding that the interest rate depended on global trade flows:

> [T]that which causes increase of Profit to the Borrower of Money, is the less quantity of Money, in proportion to Trade, or to the Vent of all Commodities, taken together.
>
> (SC-71)

This would then lead him to the following citation linking the quantity of money and the level of 'trade'. Here is the quotation in full:

> The natural Value of Money…depends on the whole quantity of the then passing Money of the kingdom, in proportion to the whole Trade…(i.e.) the general Vent of all…Commodities.
>
> (SC-72)

This then elucidates, and comprehensively, Locke's notion of natural interest. Furthermore, the following point must be emphasised: the extreme complexity, but also the extreme rigour of a reasoning which started out from the idea of the functions of money, then from that of a contract to deploy what already appears as the first macroeconomic theory in history. Under these conditions, the impact this had on the English Parliament is understandable. Clarke reported on the matter in a letter to Locke.[26]

However, it should be remembered, as this discussion draws to an end, that this theory of natural interest was only one element of his financial analysis. It was certainly pivotal, but it only made sense when compared to a short-term analysis tracing the behaviour of financial operators. This was what Locke would do before and after this discussion in order to ascertain the notion of financial regulation. Nonetheless, it is appropriate to pause for reflection before addressing it, because Locke can only be appreciated from the ultimate political purpose of the 'Considerations'. This would involve fully integrating his philosophy.

This is the aim of this short paragraph in the guise of a preliminary conclusion.

Concluding observation: Locke's economic theory and the State of Nature

This work started by recalling the surprising attitude of a whole intellectual tradition, which had led to assimilating Locke's credit analysis with that of his 'mercantilist' opponents. The ramifications of this position had been especially noted as they blur any understanding of his financial analysis. In fact, it prevented him from thinking of a function that would be assigned to credit and that could justify the premise of its regulation.

It can be affirmed henceforth that this was nonsense, undoubtedly one of the most serious in this discipline. Since in reality, this debate has shown that (1) Locke was well aware of the weaknesses of the 'mercantilists', (2) but he had overcome them, starting from a totally revised theoretical basis focused around the idea of the contract, (3) and that this basis, through its 'realism', empowered the idea of a function – to be more precise, a function that could be assigned to credit. This is in full agreement with Keynes here who qualified him as the first macroeconomic theorist.

However, the most important point is undoubtedly elsewhere. It is in the *normative* nature of Locke's theories and even further in their philosophical anchoring – everything that has been denied. It is precisely in their anchorage in Natural Right. If this is indeed the case, nothing should prevent Locke's ideas from being approached in terms of his political philosophy from now on. On the contrary, this is the only way.

2.5.1 The State of Nature

In order to illustrate this, however, a final element needs to be introduced, underlining that Locke has been part of a particular tradition within jusnaturalism, which bears an original thesis: that there would exist in a community a State of Nature, which would 'pre-exist' the political State and determine it. '*We must consider what State all Men are naturally in*' says the first sentence of his Treatise.

Clearly, this position is central to his philosophy. It has been the subject of countless debates, difficult to summarise because there was hardly any minimal consensus. It can be said, however, that three main standpoints have emerged, which can be presented as follows:

1. The first one is *historic*. It consists in arguing that the State of Nature represented a mythical description of the way early societies existed. This was often put forward until the middle of the 20th century.

However, it has been challenged by contemporary debate which emphasised that both 'Natural' and 'political' states coexisted for Locke, particularly when he affirmed that '*the obligations of the law of nature cease not in Society*' (TCG-§135). This debate was then split up into two main standpoints:

2. A *social interpretation* that perceived this State of Nature as the depiction of social practice as it should take place independently of political law. Locke's purpose would be to judge morally of that. He could be linked to Macpherson, who would argue that Locke's aim was to legitimise the practice of capitalist accumulation. But other authors could also be mentioned, including Mitchell and of course Strauss.[27]
3. Finally a *moral, even religious* interpretation that portrayed this State of Nature as a philosophical theory intended to represent the normative principles that should regulate a society. Dunn, the most well-known, speaks about principles of religious origin:

   [T]he state of nature is a jural condition and the law which covers it is the theologically based law of nature.[28]

Simmons himself speaks about a '*moral condition of man*' which seems more in line with the Locke of the 'Considerations'.[29]

There was, therefore, more than just a nuance in these standpoints because it was the political meaning of the Treatise that was at stake. This is why commentators have often seen through Locke's interest for trade a justification for the social interpretation of the State of Nature – Vaughn, for example – but the majority of economists could be quoted here.[30] However, if there is now an outcome from this discussion, it is that it is entirely at odds with this *a priori*, and instead validates the normative view of the State of Nature – if not Dunn's, then at least Simmons'. There are two reasons for this:

- For a methodological reason first of all. The essence of the State of Nature – as modern authors understood it – is to incorporate into human reality a duality between political society and this State of Nature. For Ashcraft, this even becomes a vehicle for discussion. Now it is this duality that was encountered in this financial debate, since two levels of analysis were discerned from the outset:
  - that of financial transactions, which was clearly a matter for the political state, and which logically refers back to the idea of regulation,
  - when the realm of real transactions determined the norm to be followed.

This duality, moreover, would be maintained in all the 'Considerations', particularly in Locke's conception of money. Thus, it will be seen as justification that Locke did indeed approach the economic world in jusnaturalist terms.

- However, now it is necessary to go further by referring to the notion of *natural interest*, which *for Locke signals the existence of norm governing financial activity*. Since it seems clear that this dimension refers to the State of Nature, and that this is how Locke's 'Considerations' imagined it. It could, therefore, only be read through the moral meaning of Dunn or Simmons: a behavioural norm or alternatively a set of practices proven to this point that they have become binding norms. Likewise, the term 'consensus' could also be mentioned, which Locke would use to qualify the monopoly exercised by 'the banks' – he stated 'by consent'. It was even through this idea that Locke introduced his 'Considerations'. In fact, this term refers to the reasonable character of practitioners who would justify for Locke, this norm's legitimacy. Dunn should be quoted on this point:

Where a practice is legitimate and a role involves participation in the practice, consent to doing so and...to its responsibilities is axiomatic.[31]

There is no doubt, therefore, that there is a real coherence between Locke's economic position and the moral interpretation of the State of Nature.

> ==> This means, and this will be the last conclusion of this Chapter: that the 'Considerations' are an application of this moral model.

However, it would be going too fast to settle for such a supposition, since only one aspect of Locke's argument has been dealt with, albeit the most complex. Some essential points would be missed particularly regarding the moral framework of his theory of interest.

However, in order to do that, it is necessary to take a fresh look at the 'Considerations', but from now on focussing on its financial analysis. This is the purpose of Chapter 3.

Notes

1 Tucker-*Progress and profits...*, 1960. His misunderstanding of Dutch financial policy was regretful. It can be presumed that it prevented him from deepening his understanding of Locke. Tucker was Robinson's student.
2 Just how much did Keynes borrow from Locke? This question revived interest in the '*Considerations*' following on from the General Theory. To address it in-depth here would be to go beyond the limits of this work: however, the basic elements of this discussion will be covered.
3 On this point, see Chapter 3.
4 '*[For Locke] the rate of interest would be affected by changes in the profits of trade and industry*', Op. cit., p. 27.
5 According to Leigh, Locke had the capacity of deriving interest from the rentability of companies. in '*Locke and the QTM...*', 1991, p. 339.
6 '*The distinction between moral and technical knowledge...was made throughout the 17th.*', Op.cit., pp. 147-148
7 In particular, those of Caffentzis, Hekscher, Hegeland (quoted in Chapter 1) and even Macpherson who nevertheless emphasised Locke's quotation (Op. Cit., p. 206).
8 Misselden, '*The circle of commerce*', 1971 (see also Malynes [1973]).
9 Manley, '*Usury at 6% examined*', 1669.
10 '*[It] is as equitable...as receiving Rent for Land...notwithstanding the Opinion of some over-scrupulous Men*' (SC-57).
11 Schumpeter did not deny that jusnaturalist authors and thus, Locke, had a normative approach to economics. His thesis is that their analysis '*presupposed an explanatory natural law*' and could therefore be reduced to a positive analysis (Op. cit., p. 111). It is this point that is contested here.
12 '*The natural rate was an abstract norm, a criterion for judging the behaviour of individuals*' (Op. cit., p. 769).

13 '*History of England from the accession of James II*', 1855, p. 631.

14 The following criticism also applies to Diatkine, who de facto attributed Vaughan's position to Locke – hence, his refusal to accept Locke's idea of the '*double value of money*'.

15 This is a reference to the discussion started in Chapter 1. Locke takes the example of an already specific author, who sought to think the use of money as store of value. Locke's logic was therefore to show that the mercantilist aporia remained the same as long as the notion of 'monetary function' was not understood. The argument – which dates back to the 'early writings' – was also valid against cartalism.

16 It is in this precise way that we must read Keynes' formula quoted in the introduction. It is to be regretted that he did not measure what was at stake in the notion of the 'double value' of money: he merely noted its existence.

17 Op. cit., p. 206. See Chapter 5 on the theory of property.

18 It is surprising that Schumpeter opposed Locke's position to Barbon's formula – admittedly rough – comparing interest to '*capital rent*' (Op. cit., p. 329).

19 Op. cit., pp. 44–48. What was at stake for Petty *was not* a market theory, but to assess England's wealth, and namely value of land. He did this by (simple) capitalisation of the rent, making the 'life span' play a role as an operator between these two notions and comparing it with interest. The problem posed by this theory is that it created the illusion that a fall in the interest rate would increase the price of land (see Vidonne [1982]).

20 Foucault would compare this passage to a mercantilist approach (Op. cit., pp. 197–200). But wrongly so because he would confuse the function of intermediation and the nature of money in Locke's work. It could be shown that this error queries the very heart core of his argument on modern '*épistémé*'.

21 '*The vent is…the passing of commodities from one owner to another*' (SC-67). Several authors – including Vaughn – correctly described the analogy with the notion of density in physics.

22 The neo-classical version of this theory applies to the whole economy and not to a single function. Notice, however, that it is not possible to move from one to the other without a complete transformation of money. This was the point that Locke would not reach.

23 In '*Theorien über den Mehrwert*', 1976. Marx relied on the many quotations in the Treatise where Locke derived this value from labour. He would be widely followed (see Hundert : "The…Treatise…established the foundation for the modern conception of labor", in '*The Making of Homo Faber*', 1972, p. 7; see also Diemer [2008] and others). The observation is correct (TCG-§40), but Marx forgot that 'labour' had, for Locke, a *religious* dimension (Ashcraft, '*Revolutionary politics and Locke's two treatises…*', 1986, Chap. VI; see also Dunn). It excludes any quantification. However, the labour-value theory assumed this quantification as early as Smith. To attribute it to Locke is a serious mistake.

24 '*Value theory forms the basis of his whole economic writings*' (Op. cit., p. 17). By taking such a position Vaughn overlooked the internal balance of Locke's

thinking. It led her to interpret Locke as a neoclassical precursor – closely akin to Dunn's criticism [1981].

25 This was not exactly Petty's thesis, who defended free rate setting in his *Quantulumcumque* [1906]. The way in which he defended his standpoint on the value of capital could, however, easily be used as a defence of lowering interest rate.

26 In De Beer (Op. cit., 23/01/1692).

27 Strauss, *Natural Right and History,* 1954; Mitchell, *Locke and the rise of capitalism,* 1986. For a more complete vision, see Onur [2011].

28 Dunn, '*The political thought of...Locke*', 1969, p. 106.

29 The important point for Simmons is the a-sociological character of the State of Nature: 'The state of nature is a moral condition...and a relational one... compatible with a wide range of social circumstances', in '*Locke's state of nature*', 1989, p. 460. On his difference with Dunn (Op. cit., p. 468).

30 These points will be discussed in more detail in Chapter 5. Note also Bouillot, '*The conflict in the Lockean State of Nature...*', 2019, or Diatkine who thought possible to read here the opposition between landowners and 'monied men'.

31 In '*Consent in the political theory...*', 1967, p. 182.

3 From savings to financial regulation

The purpose of this second discussion is to restore the political meaning of Locke's first 'Considerations' in order to understand their influence on the financial revolution. This will be built, thus, on the initial outcomes concerning interest, and an attempt will be made to demonstrate how they nurtured his financial analysis, and, beyond that, his banking regulation project. This is why the analysis of savings and their transformation through the banking sector will be emphasised, because for Locke, they will be the main elements of this regulation.

However, in order to appreciate this, it is important to remember that this text was drafted as an address to a Parliament, for a specific debate leading to a law. It will, therefore, be read as an analysis of the situation that prevailed at the time, and also as a political project, specifically a financial policy project. But, with this nuance that this reference to 'politics' was perceived in a broad sense at that time, including a strong moral dimension. This means that both this analysis and this project were carried out from the idea of a finality assigned to economic life – precisely a politico-moral finality – and which necessarily referred to Locke's philosophy.

These 'Considerations' should thus be seen as an application of this philosophy offering valuable insights. In fact, it represents the main text of this kind available today about Locke.

3.1 The moral framework of the 'Considerations'

As has already been stated, this situation, which the English Parliament was going to deal with, resulted in a shared feeling of financial shortage, which was considered to penalise trade. It will be discussed here later under 'economic growth'. This means that there was already a clear shared vision and a certain kind of comprehension of the economic world and the mechanisms that governed it. However, it also means that a majority of decision-makers made support for activity a key issue in public life: both of them already making up the core of the vision of politics that would impose itself in the 18th and 19th centuries. It is therefore important to underline that one of Locke's recurring statements was to agree with this, or even to outmatch it, by punctuating his text with very colourful illustrative expressions. Thus, for example, such passages:

> For Money [is] and as necessary to Trade, as Food is to Life.
>
> (SC–6)

> Trading is necessary for the production of wealth, and money for trading.
>
> (SC–17)

It must, therefore, be assumed that Locke adhered fully to these still new ideas, and that, as a philosopher, he associated the idea of 'moral good' with growth. Thus, that is enough to question the so-called Cambridge analysis, which made Locke appear like a conservative author at the economic level and very restrained one concerning the logic of capitalism. According to Dunn, in fact, he would the bearer of a 'radical Calvinist policy' that was basically hostile to the pursuit of profit.[1]

The answer to these authors is that while the protestant influence on Locke is unquestionable, the 'Considerations' were at odds with this Calvinist radicalism. They were much closer to the 'industrious philosophy' described by Ashcraft, which incited Locke to insist 'upon the value of human industry'.[2] They even ask the question, regardless, of their affinity with utilitarianism. These points will be reviewed in the conclusion.

However, in doing so, this all goes back to this observation that the 'Considerations' did not really disassociate themselves from the other parties involved in this debate, especially those that Locke was going to challenge. The debate was actually about a financial theme and it took place at a very high and even rather technical level. What was at stake was precisely the effect on growth of a legal lowering of interest, and there is agreement that Locke led two discussions, but of unequal importance.

1. Firstly, he came up against Petty's rationalism,[3] which linked interest to the present value of capital – in this case land – and therefore wanted interest to go down in order to support its price. This was seen in Chapter 2.

This debate, however, had little impact on the banking system. This is why, while it was central to the 'early writings', it was watered down in the 'Considerations', with Locke only responding to it in the course of his market analysis.

2. Moreover, he came up against Child's[4] financial analysis, which was based on the financial offer: his thesis being that England had significant savings, but that high interest rates discouraged people from investing in companies (see also Chapter 2):

> This seeming scarcity of money proceeds from the trade of bankering...most men as soon as they [have] a sum of 50£ send it to the goldsmith.
>
> (Op. cit., p. XLVI)

Hence his plea for lowering interest.

3.1.1 The methodology for this chapter

Locke was not opposed to Child on savings, as he even shared some of the latter's misgivings about banking efficiency. But he was opposed on two very precise points, which will be revealing of his own convictions:

- Through the rigour of his approach to the supply of money first of all, which would enable him to insist on the *moral dimension* of savings whereas only the economic dimension was previously considered (paragraph 3.2).
- Through his financial analysis then because of its theoretical foundations.

It was notably on this second point that the discussion coalesced, taking on two dimensions: (1) a *critical* dimension where Locke would contest Child's stance by explaining its counter-productive character – this was the meaning of the first arguments of the 'Considerations' – and (2) an analytical dimension where he would propose his own analysis of how banks should function, providing the foundation for his theory on regulation – see paragraphs 3.4 and 3.5.

However, this would be a complex analysis, since it was inevitably based on his theory of interest, and would consequently leverage the whole of his economic analysis. It would principally be a *normative* analysis, inexorably restating the normative dimension of this theory of interest. However, this is an aspect that has been not fully understood through interpretation. This will lead to preface it with a methodological observation, making it possible to contextualise its theoretical and political stake (paragraph 3.3 "the normative dimension of financial analysis").

A final aside should be opened to contextualise the interpretations that have been made of these passages. They will be described as modest, since as has already been stated, there has been very little discussion on the subject of regulation – and above all, as highly differentiated. For it cannot be asserted, strictly speaking, that Locke's financial analysis has been neglected; several authors have referred to it, strongly emphasising its critical dimension against 'the banks' (Ashcraft and Kelly). It will even be mentioned so as to underline Locke's opposition to the money creation model (Wennerlind). Anyway this was carried out in such a one-sided way that it distorted the meaning of Locke's views. For that reason, these authors' views will be discussed.

On the other hand, the interpretation was more precise on the theme of savings, as several authors noted the role it played for Locke. Many speak of 'accumulation' in a Marxist way[5] which is not unacceptable, but introduces real bias (Onur, Macpherson). It is, in fact, the moral interpretation of this saving that has been problematic. Therefore, with the exception of Ashcraft, little connection has been made between the 'Considerations' and the theory of property, which nevertheless addresses the same issue. This theme will be reviewed with him, and the philosophical issue of the 'Considerations' will be reviewed again at the end of this chapter. This saving theme should now be addressed.

3.2 Savings at the heart of growth

What could be called Locke's growth theory is actually a long-term argumentation that focused on the factors of supply of funds to companies: this supply is deemed to be scarce and less than financing needs. For the sake of clarity, it must be distinguished from the short-term problem posed by the problematic *availability* of these funds. This point will only be addressed at the end of the paragraph.

Under this caveat, Locke's growth theory would only have a long-term objective, as Leigh and, in some respect, Macpherson have pointed out.

3.2.1 Growth factors – foreign trade and financial savings

However, it is important to be precise and to note that a theory of this type had to be a calculation, which at that time was a sign of sophisticated reasoning. However, from Locke's point of view it could only be achieved in political terms, in other words, by identifying the ultimate factors that weighed on the supply, and which would be potentially feasible to regulate. So, it was not simply a question of measuring an economic quantity as a Petty would have done, but an investigative analysis as can be understood today. This is why Locke would again innovate in relation to his contemporaries by adopting the same 'marginal' reasoning that was observed in relation to his theory of interest – so that his theory can be read as a sophisticated differential calculus, the issue being to assess the factors of growth (or contraction) of the money supply. It would be based on three points:

1. Locke would first of all establish the existence of a stability in the quantity of money necessary for trade operations at a given level of activity. A theory that he formulates in this way:

    > [T]herefore ready Money must be constantly exchang'd for Wares and Labour, or follow within a short time after…This shews the necessity of some Proportion of Money to Trade.
    >
    > (SC-33)

This statement astounded its (few) commentators. Astounded not by its content, which is still accepted today, but by the care that was taken to demonstrate it. Indeed, Locke went as far as to estimate the working capital required at each stage of the economic cycle, and this was compared to the first formalisation of a TEE[6] in an economy (SC, pp. 33–43). In the same guise as this passage:

> [B]etween the Landlord and Tenant there must necessarily be…a quarter of the Yearly Revenue…constantly in their hands.
>
> (SC-38)

Without exaggerating, this could be considered as an anticipation of the monetary circuit theory.

This standpoint, however, needs to be seen as essential, particularly from a logical point of view, in order to quantify the factors of supply growth. For it made it possible to argue that any increase/decrease in money circulation directly impacted money supply, which greatly narrowed the analysis of the factors that explained it. For this reason, and once this point was made, Locke would focus on the variables that explained this variation. Literally, they are the ones that would constitute his theory. Namely:

2. Foreign trade, which would result in an increase in money circulation, due to the increase in the trade balance or its decrease. The reason is obvious and was generally accepted:

> [B]y Commerce Silver is brought in only by an over-ballance of Trade.
>
> (FC-16)

3. Then, it was the financial savings that Locke would address through its exact opposite of *private debt*. He must be quoted directly, but this point deserves an explanation:

> The Natural Interest of Money is raised two ways: First, When the Money of a Country is but little in proportion to the Debts of the Inhabitants one amongst another.
>
> (SC-10,11)

Indeed, what is called 'saving' in economics is an action aimed at increasing one's own wealth, most often through more work and less consumption. Locke would talk about *'general frugality and industry'*. The theoretical concept, by extension, is aimed at the result of this action. But at the time, it was still difficult to distinguish the type of wealth that was being saved, particularly in its monetary dimension. Thus, the different forms of savings were treated indifferently. However, Locke, and this is an essential point, did not share this view. He considered that savings should be distinguished according to their use, and this means precisely: whether they were used productively or unproductively. This relates to the very core of his political theory. Consequently, the appreciation of Ashcraft – who saw that it was an essential issue[7] – should be adhered to:

> [Second treatise] has this intentional objective: to provide a defense of 'the industrious' and trading part of the nation…against the idle, improductive…owners.
>
> (Op. cit., p. 264)

Nonetheless, it must also be regretted that Ashcraft was not precise enough. Since what was at stake, from Locke's standpoint, was as much this idea of saving as its *dynamic*, the very fact that it could be reinvested in the economic cycle. This is even a crucial point for this work, because it is connected to the theoretical notion of 'store value' linking it further to the theory of property – see Chapter 1. However, the clearest way to illustrate this is to revisit the debate with Petty concerning the analysis of the price of capital. Its theoretical foundations have already been expounded.

3.2.2 The debate with Petty and the political issue of savings

It is indeed very common in economics to associate capital value with interest rates and Petty is credited with the first quantified formalisation of this relation. However, this standpoint had the twofold disadvantage of confusing the value of capital with its market price, and of allowing the market to be regulated, for example, by pushing down interest. This was what Locke would contest, as was seen previously, with the idea of a 'supply price' for capital, which was different from its value:

> [T]his is that then which makes land dear, plenty of buyers, and but few sellers.
>
> (SC-61)

This debate therefore had an important theoretical dimension, but it is the way Locke defended his standpoint that is important here.

For when he spoke of a price for land, it was not about comparing this capital to a commodity, as seen previously, but describing a specific market in which *savings* were the key factor of demand – more specifically: savings resulting from commercial activity. It was, therefore, investment stemming from these savings that explained ultimately the price of capital. Locke should be cited once again because the way he described this phenomenon is emblematic of his general standpoint:

> [W]hen the thriving Tradesman has got more, than he can…employ, his next Thoughts are to look out for a Purchase, to leave to their children, but it must be a Purchase in the Neighbourhood…not [taking] him off from the Engagements of his Calling.[8]
>
> (SC-61)

In fact, this passage illustrates a fundamental theme in Locke's economic thought. It is the idea that investment, or better still, *the dynamic of savings* was an essential factor in economic activity, if not the main one. It was therefore the focus of Locke's attention, but he did so in a distinctive way: by approaching the individual dimension in his theory of property – this will be better perceived in Chapter 5 – when the 'Considerations' would approach it particularly from a collective point of view. They therefore focused on the macroeconomic dimension, in other words, its socialisation through the financial aspect.

However, such distinctions were still unclear to economists, and it is not certain that Locke himself had all the theoretical concepts to explain it.[9] That is why he approached financial savings from the perspective of *private debt*, which is technically speaking his exact opposite. *On this basis, his growth theory would merely* link the development of trade to money supply and thus to the two elements that have just been identified: *foreign trade and financial savings.*

3.2.3 Primacy attributed to financial savings and its moral dimension

However, a final point – but very rarely underlined – needs to be mentioned. For out of these two factors, indeed from a purely accounting aspect, the first was undoubtedly the most important. This is why Locke would join most of his contemporaries in making foreign trade a key factor in the wealth of a nation – even if at the expense of others. In that way, which is a 'doctrinal' way, Locke was indeed a mercantilist author:

> [T]he over-balancing of Trade between us and our Neighbours, must inevitably carry away our Money, and quickly leave us Poor, and exposed.
>
> (SC-14)

On the other hand, and this is essential, he would not adopt a protectionist standpoint, and no doubt he was not alone on this point – see quotations hereafter.[10] In fact, he considered that such measures were ineffective, or easily misused, which in terms of analysis had significant consequences. Since it meant that the factors explaining the growth of foreign trade were *the same* as those relating to trade in general and that they were linked to the availability of 'money'. This was hardly questionable at that time. But, this led to consider that foreign trade *was not an independent variable*, that is, it depended on the supply of money in the same way as other activities. This is particularly implied in the following quotation:

> He that wants a Vessel, rather than lose his Market, will…and find ways to do it…though the Rate were limited by a Law.
>
> (SC-11)

It would be said today that it was an endogenous[11] variable.

His standpoint on savings, however, was completely different, which explains his insistence on this point. For these savings were principally the result of human behaviour, and read here as *moral behaviour.* He described them as the convergence of two practices, the sound management of property, which he insisted on at length:

> As if the vertue…of our ancestors…was brought in fashion…'Tis with a kingdom as with a family ([only] better husbandry keep us from sinking.
>
> (SC–117,118)

and thrift in consumption – at least not to be tempted by luxury. The terms he used were unambiguous and just quoted here:

> If a neglect of Government and Religion, ill Examples, and depraved Education, have introduc'd Debauchery…has made it fashionable for Men to live beyond their Estates, Debts will increase and multiply.
>
> (SC–84,85)

Starting from this point, and it is what matters here, Locke would make these savings a structuring variable in his analysis. It could therefore be interpreted as a 'propensity to save' which obviously needed to be encouraged, but which also included a financial dimension: 'it is [necessary] to encourage lending' (SC-14).

Then, if looked at from a political point of view, financial savings would be the main factor of economic growth – beyond, of course, the general determinant of 'human industry'. This is the conclusion that must be drawn from this discussion, and this would, of course, have an impact on his vision of the financial system.

3.2.4 The common thread of the 'Considerations': the transformation of savings

For what must be understood is that the importance taken by these savings necessarily raises a related question, which is their transformation into a supply of funds for businesses. This makes sense, and thus it is where Locke's financial analysis should be mentioned.

Hence, as was specified from the outset, this transformation was problematic at the time, due to what has been described as 'banking speculation' and its lack of regulation. This 'speculation' resulted especially in a recurrent loss of saved funds to the detriment of the supply to companies. It was therefore quite rational for Locke to channel his 'Considerations' towards a critical analysis of the system established by the banks. In fact, it was a question of making *the efficiency of this system* a specific factor of growth, and it can already be assumed that this analysis could lead to *policy* proposals on its regulation.

However, in doing so, Locke would come up against a methodological difficulty, which few observers have highlighted, and which concerned the normative dimension of such a discussion. It is by expounding it that the cutting edge of his financial analysis will be attained.

3.3 The normative dimension of financial analysis

It is important to underline that the concepts used regularly to describe the financial world – such as 'financial system', 'function' or even 'speculation' – are not empirical concepts, as is often believed. Or rather, they are only empirical *subject to* the existence of regulatory structures such as the one that would appear in England, which *standardise in reality* banking behaviour. It is actually this standardised behaviour that is empirically observed and conceptualised[12] by theory. This is why, for an economist, financial analysis must be stated as at least partially normative.

It must be understood, however, that at that time these subtleties were unknown. As stated abundantly, theory was based on the market model, and the backbone of the market is to provide a system without finality. So, if certain bank behaviour could be observed, as proven by the arbitrage theories, and even if there was a real distrust of them, there was a major difficulty in evaluating them at a theoretical level through an inability for normative reasoning. This explains why there was no real theory on the role of banks before Locke.

Henceforth, it is now known that Locke mastered that kind of thinking. He mastered this through his Natural Right approach, where he could simultaneously argue the idea of a norm for financial practices – derived from natural interest – and the need for the law to comply with that norm. It was therefore possible for him to approach this matter in a coherent way, and he did so in two phases, which would then constitute his core argument:

1. An analytical phase which would consist in qualifying the banks' behaviour which was unthinkable at that time.

Therefore, it can be said that he resumed and *completed* his theory of interest. But, it must be pointed out, above all, that he was then describing a banking function. This will be covered in paragraph 3.4 "From the analysis of banking speculation to the theme of regulation".

2. This function itself referring to a political level where it would become a guide for action. The expression through which he introduced his recommendations is cited below:

[D]o I say there is no law at all to regulate interest; I say not so.

(SC-102)

But, to achieve this, and this is the final point, he still had to defend this analysis in relation to the authors he was opposing, and he would do so on two levels:

1. He would be extremely uncompromising, first of all, with the followers of the money creation model, whom he reproached for ignoring the reality of credit, and in particular, that the debt clearing always referred to cash, read: to species.[13] It may be interesting to quote him here, because the tone as well as the ethos bears a very close resemblance to Paterson. This was, of course, no coincidence:

    [F]or nothing will pay debts but money or moneys worth which three or four lines writ in paper cannot be.

    (SC-29)

Actually, for Locke, this model would remain theoretical, and whatever some authors[14] may have asserted, this point had to be recognised. For that reason, he did not consider this in his analysis of bank behaviour.

2. For in fact, his main opponent was Child's arbitration theory, which referred to the practices of established banks. In order to challenge it, he therefore had to articulate at least three lines of reasoning, all three referring to this famous normative dimension, respectively (1) to contest Child's theoretical basis, (2) while proposing an alternative analysis, (3) to finally attain his own policy recommendations.

It was no mean task. Accordingly, it explains why the 'Considerations' opened with a long discussion on banking behaviour, which included these three levels. It can now be asserted that it would form the political heart of the discussion (SC, pp. 1–25).

3.4 From the analysis of banking speculation to the theme of regulation

Unfortunately, this analysis did not receive the attention it deserved, as much by the silence of renowned commentators (Schumpeter, Marx, Letwin and so on) – and to say the least – as by the guesswork of those who sought to comment on it (Ashcraft and Kelly). This is highly regrettable because, in reality, Locke successfully addressed all three levels. The meaning, furthermore, can be recreated in a contemporary way, that is to say, in the form of theoretical principles. There are logically three of them.

3.4.1 The banking system as a natural monopoly

1. Banking intermediation is in a monopoly position in the savings transformation cycle; and this monopoly can said to be 'natural' ('by consent').

This is Locke's first thesis and its nuanced character must be emphasised. For Locke has sometimes been credited with a one-sided attitude towards the banks which *condemned* their monopolistic character. This was Ashcraft's thesis, but implicitly also the same as Vickers or even Carey:

> [For Locke] bankers are a monopoly in the money market…as the case of engrossers of corn.
>
> (Op. cit. p. 103)

However, this was only partially the case, and by confining the analysis to that, Locke's standpoint has literally been distorted. Since Locke had a twofold position towards the banks, one that was certainly critical, but based on a recognition of their role. This was illustrated in the very first sentence of the 'Considerations' – already cited in Chapter 2 – which was directed against Child, meaning that the banking system could not be *bypassed*, as he believed. It is this duality that has been concealed.

So it is important to note that when Locke talks about this 'monopoly', he means two things. Firstly, that it was the main instrument available to savers:

> [F]or men finding the convenience of lodging their money in hands where they can be sure of it at short warning.
>
> (SC-3)

This is also illustrated by his sour remarks about these 'lazy' (SC-3) who 'rush to London' to invest their money. However, the argument went much further. Above all, it meant that this monopoly position was linked to the very practice of financial operators – savers, bankers and entrepreneurs – and that it had become central to economic life. This is why he used the term 'by consent', which, it should be remembered, contains the idea of an implicit agreement among the operators, but is binding as a norm in a community:

[A] kind of Monopoly by consent, has put this general Commodity into a few Hand.

That made Child's position untenable because, in fact, it meant accepting the banks as *a fact*. Although, if a proof of this nuanced approach was needed, it was to be seen in the language Locke used here.

For in the whole of this discussion, and unlike the one on savings, Locke never considered it on pure moral grounds. Though, he would follow the only *reason*, read: the rational behaviour of operators. It was, first of all, the logic of this rationality that he would describe, leaving criticism of behaviour to just a few certain bankers' clients.

3.4.2 The asymmetry of skills and banking rationality

Hence, through such an approach, Locke introduced an absolutely new element into economic thinking, which necessarily shifted the conditions of the debate: that of differences in rationality between operators in the same sector. This point referred to his second argument.

2. This banking monopoly is characterised by a structural imbalance between the operators in the financial system, linked to the *asymmetry* of their skills. Contemporary terms are deliberately used here to show Locke's headway at the theoretical level.[15]

To illustrate this, it can be stated that according to Locke, the banker had, through his activity, a better knowledge of the conditions of a loan than the customer, being familial, for instance, with the natural rate. However, most importantly, he took advantage of this by inducing a recurrent distortion in the setting of rates. This has been amply explained in Chapter 2.

It was this distortion that Locke would condemn in the form of a gap between the rate applied and the natural rate. This is why he was always extremely precise in his judgements, stressing that this contrast in skills was mainly to the *disadvantage* of savers, who were not accustomed to this type of action. The commercial borrower, in contrast, would know about profitability (SC-1,19). Furthermore, it must be added that Locke would not always be 'tender' in his judgements. Thus, two cases will be cited that reflect his point of view:

[W]hen you have taken it down by Law to that Rate, no body will think of having more than Four per Cent…though those who have need of Money…pay Seven or Eight.

Most of those that had not the Skill, put it in the Bankers Hands.

(SC-6,8)

Thus, if it was true that banking intermediation was unavoidable, then this skills distortion induced some major phenomena, and this was where the heart of his criticism lay.

3.4.3 The inefficiency of the banking system

Since this distorsion authorised or even stimulated monopolistic and, what could only be described as speculative behaviour. However, what should be emphasised are:

3. The economic consequences of such phenomena, namely, that they were influencing the transformation of savings. That was the key point of the demonstration because it meant that this asymmetry was a *major cause* of the shortage of money that was being felt.

However, it was a cause that could be acted upon. This is why Locke would illustrate this point with a series of examples taken from the hypothetical case of a drop in interest. He would describe, respectively,

• The 'liquidity preference' mechanism, a term that was coined by Keynes, and which reflected the tendency for savers to disinvest when faced with low returns. This obviously reduced the money supply:

This loss to the mony'd Men will be a prejudice to Trade: Since it will discourage Lending at such a disproportion of Profit, to Risque.

(SC-14)[16]

It should be mentioned that Locke borrowed this analysis from mercantilist writers (Manley[17]).

• The underinvestment that this implied, due to the excessive profits made, and this was a very sensitive point. For it has to be said that the speculative opportunities were such at that time that excessive profits resulted in an increase in speculation: often by hoarding[18] practices that will be at stake in his debate with Lowndes. Further, consequently, there was a decline in the supply to companies:

> For the Bankers paying at most but Four per Cent…and receiving from Six to Ten per Cent. or more, at that low Rate could be content to have more Money lye dead by them, than now when it is higher…[it] means there would be less Money…in Trade, and a greater Scarcity.
>
> (SC-7)[19]

•   Locke would focus on the phenomena of disparity in the distribution of credit, inherent in this monopolistic culture:

> [C]urrent of running Cash, which now takes its course almost all to London.
>
> (SC-103)

This point would be particularly close to his heart, as he saw it as a fracture in the fair treatment of entrepreneurs. It was, moreover, on this theme that the *only (semi)public* criticism he would make of the Bank of England appeared but which he limited to his political friends: Locke's thesis being that equity in the distribution of funds should be guaranteed by the Parliament. He would even go so far as to point out the risk of a drift of the executive power because of its privileged position regarding the Bank.[20]

> It becomes the wisdom of Parliament…to consider how money might be better distributed into the country. [21]

These were undoubtedly very real risks. It should be noted, however, that this position was subsequent to the creation of the Bank. Above all it concerned only on the downstream side of the financing process, when the main problem was the mobilisation of savings. This explains why he maintained his alliance with the Bank during the monetary reform. It symbolically closes his analysis of the functioning of the banking system.

This is, therefore, a very thorough analysis, especially when compared to those that preceded Locke. Since in reality, it traces the entire process that leads from saving to making savings available. It must, therefore, be considered as a core part of the 'Considerations', the essence of his message to Parliament. However, it is also an analysis whose normative dimension must be stressed, and this especially must be done before addressing the political considerations.

3.4.4 From the role of finance to its necessary regulation

It is indeed important to remember, at the end of this discussion, that the behaviour described in relation to banks and the judgments made were all based on a specific theory – that is, the theory of interest – whose normative nature has to be recognised. This has been explained at length. This banking analysis was therefore, in terms of method, of a special nature. Though it appeared to be empirical, this empiricism was guided by a norm, and the meaning of this norm no longer remains a mystery. It obviously referred to the idea of an efficient transformation of savings.

It can, therefore, be stated that a *function* for the banks has been described at the same time as Locke explained the abuses in banker behaviour. These points have been sufficiently underlined so as draw a new conclusion. In fact, and if its theoretical and political dimensions are now consolidated:

> ==> Then the primary meaning of the 'Considerations' appears to be the description of this *banking function*, and a plea for a better transformation of savings.

This is the conclusion that can be deduced from this discussion, which noticeably refers back to the political proposals that Locke will make. For what is to say that through this function the key policy-making aspects were being depicted? That the target of such political action was being described? That appears to make sense.

It is, therefore, quite logical that Locke concluded this long analysis with recommendations for action, and that these recommendations were aimed at *bringing practice into line with the norm*. In the end, it was simply a matter of consistency.

However, an ultimate difficulty needs to be addressed here, which has to do with the way in which these conclusions have been contemplated by Locke's readers. Here it is.

3.5 Banking regulation and the general interest

It is indeed difficult to contest that Locke concluded his 'Considerations' with a well-founded proposal for the regulation of the banking system – this being supplemented by tax recommendations, but which are not the subject of this work. Nonetheless, the fact is that there were very few commentators who barely mentioned these recommendations (Tucker and Kelly), and only one did so from an analytical point of view, seeking to make economic sense of them, Kelly. Gratitude goes out to him. However, unfortunately, he did so without understanding their theoretical foundations, and by studying them so narrowly, he interpreted them as a usury draft bill – that is, legislation fixing interest at a maximum:

> Were the legal rate close to the natural, the public would benefit…
> however the establishment of the latter's monopoly … makes it
> necessary to impose a legal maximum.
>
> (Op. cit., p. 73)

Such an idea is really surprising and, dare it be said, visibly misguided.
Since it is hard to see how a text of this importance and intended to
challenge the drop in interest could lead to a proposal to…limit it. There
is a clear contradiction here.

However, this analysis had a de facto meaning, which must be
mentioned because of the privileged role of its author in the literature on Locke. It should be interpreted, in fact, as a denial: that Locke's
proposals can be seen as referring to the contemporary meaning of regulation. On this basis, there was no link whatsoever with the financial
revolution.

3.5.1 The historical formulation of the idea of banking regulation

That is being contested here for two reasons. On the one hand, because
by attaining the notion of a banking function, Locke clearly had the capacity to think this regulation through. He alone had this capacity while
his contemporaries could only think about administrating interest rates.
On the other hand, especially because the illustration he provided fully
justifies this judgement. It can be presented in five points:

1. Locke would first of all set aside his own proposal on the laws against
   usury, which he approved in principle but were not his subject matter.
   That is already an answer to Kelly:

   > [W]here Contract has not settled it between the Parties, the Law
   > might give a Rule.
   >
   > (SC-103)

2. However, and most importantly, it would reaffirm the norm of the
   natural rate, which it would seek to evaluate at length (to judge that
   the market rate at the time was consistent):

   > It would therefore perhaps, bring down the Rate of Money to
   > the Borrower, and certainly distribute it better to the Advantage of
   > Trade in the Country, if the legal Use were kept pretty near to the
   > natural.
   >
   > (SC-103)

His main purpose being to affirm two types of principles for banking activity which would be formulated in two stages:

1. By respecting company's margins: *'such Bounds should not on the one side quite Eat up the Merchants, and Tradesman's Profit, and discourage their Industry.* (SC-104) and
2. By rewarding the risk taken by the saver *'nor on the other hand so low, as should hinder Men from Risquing'*-(SC-104)

    Finally, and this is the last point, Locke would argue the need for fairness in money distribution

Hence, it is from this composition that Locke's proposal needs to be evaluated. However, in the context of the 'Considerations', it is easy to interpret.

3.5.2 Approaching the Bank of England?

Since this was obviously only a first draft, it was difficult to be more precise. However, the spirit of the proposal is clear. It consisted of seeking to adapt the banking system – namely, to adapt it to its function – subject to only one reservation, fairness. This was the meaning behind the comment on the attractiveness of the City. It was, therefore, a question of combining fairness in the circulation of savings and the efficiency of its transformation by the banks. So it can be verified that these principles are indeed those that contemporaries understand by the word 'regulation' – at least up to the neo-liberal period:

> ==> So, it is this idea that must be retained from this study: that Locke did indeed propose a coherent regulatory project, as a conclusion to his 'Considerations'.

It was even the only project that had been drafted with those concerns in mind, before the creation of the Bank of England – at least in known publications. It will therefore conclude now this discussion.

But this conclusion has to be measured in importance.

Since the question being asked in this work is that of a historical event – the creation of the first Central Bank – which has been pinpointed as illustrating this idea of regulation. Hence, the fact that Locke himself defended it, and that he did so on an official occasion, takes on a special meaning: it raises the question of the relationship between these two events. Not directly, of course, because Locke's power of influence cannot be presumed, but merely in the coherence that appears between a political decision – that of authorising the Bank – and the thinking that visibly anticipated it. How should this link between Locke's position and the creation of the Bank of England be interpreted? And what does this tell us about the creation of the Bank of England?

Such questions obviously arise and they will become the real conclusion from this reading of the 'Considerations'. The remainder of this work will set about answering these questions. However, this cannot be done in terms of substance without introducing the subject of *money*, which dominated Locke's concerns from 1694 onwards. Chapter 4 is particularly devoted to present this subject.

However, if this analysis is correct, it calls for a final reflection, which relates less to the economic scope than to its strictly philosophical dimension.

Concluding observation: general interest and social interest in Locke's political thinking

Indeed, it has been emphasised from the outset of this discussion that the debate surrounding the financial system referred to the principles of Locke's philosophy. It could even be presumed that this financial debate could shed light on these principles.

Nevertheless, it is true to say that these principles are today widely debated, at least those on which his famous Treatise of Government was based. It must be reminded how because Locke was not only a philosopher, but also a key protagonist in the political arena. This has been mentioned on every page of this work. This twofold dimension has thus posed a real problem of interpretation. Since the spontaneous tendency has been to interpret this author with one of these dimensions in mind. Was Locke a philosopher? Or was he first of all a political actor? In fact, this question structures the interpretation. It leads to relativising the context of his thinking, either seeing him as a philosopher, or to overinterpreting it in the opposite case.

Two types of answer can be identified, but by a huge oversimplification.

Historically speaking, consensus has made Locke a forerunner of utilitarian philosophy, be it that of JS Mill or that of Bentham. The reason for this was that Locke made *economics* a central element of his thinking and that there was also a common reference to his political liberalism. This explained, among other things, why the main philosophers of utilitarianism have themselves laid claim to Locke. They were followed by other interpreters, for instance, Bonar [1893], Sabine [1945] or even Chalk,[22] whose influence was strong at their time.

However, this position has been strongly criticised in recent decades, particularly with regard to this idea of political actor. The predominant theory today is that of the primacy of the context, which would explain Locke's political thinking. Some would go so far as to disqualify his philosophy: 'to speak of him as a political philosopher is inappropriate', said Laslett of his Treatise. However, the commentator who best fitted this position is undoubtedly Ashcraft, who presented Locke's political position as a social bias: he would have supported the struggle of an industrious alliance against the landed aristocracy. Ashcraft would even go as far as to argue that this one-sided approach would have determined the political content of his writings. He would then speak of class struggle in this context:

> This remark is part of a muted critique of landowners that runs as a leitmotif throughout the Considerations.
>
> (Op. cit., p. 267)

Thus, the question that needs to be asked concerns the relevance of this standpoint.

This cannot be approved however, and it can even be stated as making no sense at all. For it is not a question here of Locke's personal affinities – what Ashcraft wrote about is inspiring – but of the meaning behind his views and, in particular, their *moral* signification. It is precisely a question of deciding whether Locke retained the moral position of Natural Right – which has a universal dimension – or whether he substituted it with a circumstantial bias: the idea being, of course, that he would have assigned a moral behaviour to a social category. Since from this point of view, however, the 'Considerations' are clear, there can be no doubt about them. Not only does morality play an unambiguous role, as was witnessed in the case of savings, but the references are always transversal to social groups: which excludes Ashcraft's point of view. It is 'property management' that is being referred to, its quality that is being assessed, and not the status of the owners. If further proofs were needed, it should be perceived in the following quotation where Locke opposed two types of behaviour, that of the father and the son:

> If the Owner be a better Husband, and contenting himself with his Native Commodities…[it will] be so much Richer. He dies, and his Son succeeds…that cannot Dine without Champane and Burgundy…and the stock of his father will be quickly brought to an end.
>
> (SC-27)

Is it possible to be more opposed to the idea of social bias? The answer is actually in the question as, in fact, it applies to all the social interpretations of Locke's standpoint.[23]

But if this is the case, can a utilitarian interpretation be justified? Yes and no. 'Yes', in so far as it is emphasised that Locke's moral stance was that of a philosopher and a philosopher of economics. 'No', if it is recalled that the essence of utilitarianism was also in the affirmation of individualism, in the fact that for this school of thought, the general interest was only the convergence of individual interests. This is well known:

> The interest of the community then…what is it? the sum of the interests of the several members who compose it.[24]

Now, it is this individualist point of view that is contested here, and even if it has been accepted by contemporary authors – including Dunn.[25] Though it has just been seen, the essence of Locke's political proposal was normative, it was to regulate the financial system, to optimise the savings cycle. Since what are these topics if not an obligation of *general interest?*[26] An obligation that channelled individual interest? Since for Locke, norms were the result of human practices, but once adopted – even implicitly – they had a binding aspect. Locke was very precise:

> Private mens' interests ought not thus to be neglected, nor sacrificed to anything but the manifest advantage of the Publick.
>
> (SC–13)

It must, therefore, be concluded that Locke did not share the individualism of the utilitarians. Not that he sought to curb commercial freedom, but for him this freedom most often had a positive relationship with the general interest. In any case, it had to take second place to the general interest.

This is, of course, a vital lesson learnt. Since it was well known that the question of freedom was at the heart of Locke's political analysis. From this point of view, it necessarily prompts an examination of his best-known policy, that of money.

Notes

1 Dunn, for example: '*Differentiation in wealth leads…to a decline in the moral quality of social life under stress of the increasing motives for envy*' (Op. cit., p. 118).
2 In '*Revolutionary politics and Locke's two treatises*', 1986, p. 263.

3   We follow Keynes here, even though Culpeper or Child could be spoken of. For it was Petty who drew up the best definition of the present value of capital. But the name is of little importance here. On the link between Petty's theory and interest rate, see the discussion in Chapter 2.

4   Child was an officer of the East India Company, which illustrates the conflicts of interest underlying this debate with Locke. The theoretical level forbids, however, that these conflicts determined the two authors' standpoints.

5   Which means here 'accumulation of capital' and not of money.

6   French economic indicators.

7   See also Macpherson: *'[For Locke] the purpose of capital was not to provide a consumable income....but to beget further capital by profitable investment'* (Op. cit., p. 207).

8   This is the only passage where Locke's economic texts explicitly endorsed M. Weber's clothes. It appears, however, to be quite illustrative. On the other hand, there is nothing in these texts that refers to the theme of predestination.

9   Modern modelling of savings depends on a homogeneous understanding of income that includes both wages and profits. This homogeneousness was still foreign to Locke.

10   *'Nor will the Act of Navigation hinder their coming...many, who go for English Merchants...[being] but Dutch Factors, and Trade for others'* (SC-22); *'By the Discourse I have had in other Countries...Masters of ships take a great Liberty in their Custom-house Oaths'* (SC-5).

11   It could be argued that Locke would occupy from 1696 onwards an expert role on the Board of Trade which would be close to the contemporary 'industrial policies' (Eltis). Then, protectionism could be mentioned as it is not sure that Locke did have a theory on this subject.

12   Hence Keynes's argument to show the endogenous character of saving: *'no one can save without acquiring an asset...'* (Op. cit., p. 81). This argument only makes sense here if it is based on the existence of an organised and regulated financial system (see paragraph 3.4 on Locke's opposite analysis).

13   What Locke criticised, precisely, was the illusion of 'credit lines' that would pay off deficits without having to use metal or species for the operations of compensation. This is sufficiently conclusive to underline the unrealism of this banking model.

14   Wennerlind, for instance, who would have a hard time understanding the opposition between this model and the credit model. It explains his embarrassed silence on Locke's banking analysis, even though he correctly perceived the financial stakes of his monetary commitment.

15   See Stiglitz-Weiss [1981].

16   Keynes blamed Locke for ignoring that *'the preference for liquidity can vary'*. This is true but not very appropriate for the issues discussed here.

17   At 4% the rate would not *'answer the hazard of lending'*, quoted by Keirn [1990].

18   Hoarding consisted of selecting the species to keep and freeze the heaviest ones: most often in bank reserves (Locke), sometimes for re-melting. The

sums hoarded were considerable; they form the horizon for future monetary debates.

19 To be compared with Keynes' position, already mentioned, which states the opposite. In fact, both arguments are equally relevant, but correspond to different regulatory contexts.

20 From a letter from Clarke and Freke, relating to an additional state loan (Op. cit. 9/04/1695).

21 During an exchange with Clarke and Freke on the Bank's initial successes, early 1695 (Op. cit. 18/02/1695).

22 '*Locke's...psychology...provided much of the intellectual foundation for the utilitarian philosophy*' in 'Natural law and the rise of economic individualism', 1951, p. 347.

23 The thesis of Diatkine and Bouillot can be cited here, who thought they saw in Locke a desire to arbitrate the opposition between 'landed interest' and 'monayed interest' (Op. cit., pp. 522, 526).

24 Bentham-Principles of moral, 1969.

25 In particular, Dunn, whose 'religious' point of view, which he attributed to Locke, was essentially individualistic.

26 Here, Tully is referred to and his distinction between exclusive and inclusive natural rights, the latter being morally binding. This is close to Locke's conception (Op. cit., chap III).

4 Excursus

From the credit function to the institution of money

The question being asked in this work concerns the role played by Locke in the financial revolution – his contribution as a philosopher – and at this stage in the discussion, it is already a very advanced question.

Since, as has been stated from the very first step, the decisive point of this revolution was in the Bank of England's choice to be set up on the basis of *credit*, when the dominant model at the time was deposits. Furthermore, it positioned itself on a much broader basis: as an *intermediary* between a supply of funds from savers and the needs expressed at national level, notably by the State. By doing so, it found a way to influence what was not yet a financial system, namely, to regulate it. As just seen, Locke's project was built along these lines, and he did so in a coherent way, justifying every step of his reasoning.

It should therefore be inferred that there has been an alignment, and that beyond his role as a shareholder, there was indeed an issue of mutual concern with the Bank of England.

However, this is still far from a conclusion.

4.1 The three banking models and the creation of the Bank of England

The fact of citing alignment does not necessarily mean similarity between the two projects. In fact, Locke's standpoint was in a macroeconomic field, and was able to think about the *finality* of credit and he was even in favour of regulation by law. As for the Bank's project, the 'Paterson' project, it remained pragmatic. However, that does not change the issue behind this agreement; instead, it would tend to enlighten it.

Since this was here *upstream* of a political decision, of the very act that would create the Bank. This point now heralds a return to the initial discussion.

Indeed, it should be remembered that the Bank of England appeared at the same time as numerous other projects and attempts to create banks. Its creation was therefore initially a choice between several models which will be given a national dimension: deposits, credit or money creation. It should be underlined, however, that the choice was in favour of the only *non-intuitive* model. This could only be contemplated when based on a complex argument, capable of demonstrating its function. So it was in this context that Locke's contribution should be appreciated. It was a rational justification of the model defended by the Bank of England, and supported by the English government.

The conclusion is then obvious: whatever means were used to influence decision-makers, Locke's 'Considerations' provided a major contribution to its creation.

4.2 Towards monetary reform

However, if this is the case, this result obviously exposes a second question, that of Locke's subsequent contribution to this revolution. This is what must now be analysed. Since, as was indicated at the outset, the Bank of England was not the result of a single decision, but of a whole process that ended in 1697, which was quite a long time for such a choice. It is also well known that this period was a troubled one, marked both:

1. By increased competition between the three models, particularly at the time of the creation of the Land Bank, in April 1696, but on which consensus was already reached at the end of 1695;
2. But also by the worsening of the monetary crisis, which would bring about the largest reform in English history.

The monetary crisis of 1694/1696 was the *heightening* of a looming crisis, of which the most telling would be the appearance of an overpricing of market silver bullion compared to species – 20% in 1695. There was also heavy discounting on the pound (–20% in Amsterdam). This was characterised by the systematic clipping of silver coins and the resulting massive speculation: essentially the hoarding and export of molten coins.[1] Thus, it must be analysed as the failure of the State to curb this phenomenon.

Silver coins were estimated at 68% and at 77%, hammered coins[2] (that could be clipped). The average level of metal is estimated as follows: 1689: 84.0%, 1691:78.9%, 1692: 72.9%; 93: 66.9%; 1694: 60.1%; 1695: 50.6%; 1696: 45% (Kelly)

There was also a huge emergence of counterfeit money.

Tension in money circulation was perceptible quite early on (Locke, Macaulay), but for a long time contained because of the Treasury's choice in accepting the wrong money. On the other hand, financial arbitrages appear to be becoming widespread. Other information and the role of gold are discussed in the text.

This crisis has been widely documented by Horsefield, Li[3] and Kelly; its main features are presented in the box above. It should be recalled that although it still had a moderate impact on the circulation of money – but due to supportive political action – it had a strong impact on its *store value*, as illustrated by the premium on bullion; and through this, it must precisely be heard: the confidence in the ability of money *to store* and *restore its value at term*. From the Bank of England's point of view, it was this confidence that had to be *regained* because of its major impact on lending – a view also shared by Wennerlind.[4] This explains the *two* measures taken on this occasion, which would be summarised by speaking of a *State guarantee* on the store value of money. Being respectively:

1. Recalling species for recoinage, which meant realigning their metallic content, and in a lasting way. It would be done mostly through the refusal by the Treasury to accept any clipped coin (May 1696);
2. and, a strict monetary control policy in order to eradicate fraud and speculation. This point has been the subject of recent research highlighting the link of continuity with the Reform (Desmedt[5], Caffentzis and Wennerlind[6]).

Such measures, and it is important to point out, created a separation for such a time when a century-old tradition was to gamble on the circulation of money. Perhaps this is also the origin of the first implementation 'failures'. However, that is not the point. It is first and foremost the *institutional* dimension of this reform, since the rules for managing money were going to be *changed* – and would be changed for a long time to come. Indeed, the reform is seen as the origin of the gold standard. However, it is also in the financial consequences of this action and, in particular, in the thorough *restructuring* of assets that the reform brought about. Since by affecting the balance between species and metal, the relative value of contracts in relation to species – and notably claims – was inevitably altered. The balance between an emerging financial system and money was thus affected, and for a long time to come. The importance of the choice of the money's par value…

3 ...and the *advantage it offered for the model of credit* should therefore be gauged. Since behind an apparently technical choice, a decision was taken that laid the foundations of this emerging system.

It would only take a few months, moreover, before a coordinated management of the monetary and financial systems emerged – this was the first reform of the Bank of England (1697). Desmedt must be adhered to when he describes this event as 'the monetary foundation of the financial revolution'. So, now that is what provides the link to Locke.

4.3 The issue of the concept of money

While Locke and others warned well in advance (Macaulay), it was around 1694 that the authorities deemed the situation as dangerous.

The sequence was as follows: (1) a quasi-consensus was reached on the purpose of the reform after debates and turning to several experts (mid-1695) – specified hereafter;[7] (2) after several initiatives, a Treasury report, the so-called Lowndes report, contested this decision (July). It was notably directed against Locke as it supported the raising of the currency (around 20%).[8] (3) Chancellor Somers then appealed to Locke to contest this thesis; (4) the reform was confirmed by the government (October/November) and the Parliament (January 1696), on the basis of his written, then published intervention ('Further Considerations'); (5) its implementation is discussed in Chapter 6.

Mention should be made of Newton's action, who was appointed by the same protagonists to head the Mint (1696 and then 1699). It was he who made the transition from silver to gold.

Historians and commentators agree indeed on this point: that Locke's influence on this reform was very important, even exceptional for a philosopher. He would be the most heeded member of the expert group that was gathered before the decisions were taken. It was up to him *intuitu personae* – at the government's request – to defend the choice of the money's par value.

> ==> This was, therefore, a major contribution which can only determine its contribution to the financial revolution. The question which arises of course, is how to evaluate it.

However, what needs to be understood is that it was primarily an *intellectual* issue. Since it has already been stated from Chapter 1: monetary thinking was still very weak at that time, and this was so for a fundamental reason linked to its *material* vision of money. It was thus impossible to conceptualise its financial dimension. It should, therefore, be argued that this aporia had to be overcome and an idea capable of bearing this financial dimension had to be conceived. It means precisely: *capable of expressing* this 'store value guarantee', which was the objective of the reform. The fact is that Locke did indeed master this idea. This is what emanates, in particular, from this argument in the 'Further considerations' that he would muster against raising the par of money and where he underlined the problem of investor confidence.

> It will weaken if not totally destroy the publick faith when all that have trusted the publick...upon acts of parliament in the Million lottery, Bank act...shall be defrauded of 20 per cent of [their estate].
>
> (FC-13)

Since beyond its plausible soundness, this argument only made sense, and precisely so, if the financial conception of money was *mastered*. That Locke used it here means, therefore, a real correlation between his own conception and the transformations that money was undergoing, otherwise that they were Locke's own ideas which were being imposed on the authorities. Moreover, this is what became apparent when the money's par was chosen.

From there on, the intention of this essay becomes easier. For if that is true,

> ==> then Locke's contribution was resolved in his own conception of money. It consisted in practically re-conceptualising it; and the purpose here is just to find out how.

This is what will be at stake in the upcoming chapters.

However, the thesis being defended here goes much further. It is that Locke embraced these views as a philosopher – by relying on Natural Right – with regard to all aspects of money. He did so first from its theoretical perspective by putting forward the idea of a *conventional pledge* that was presented in the introduction, and which would allow him to rethink metal-money: this would then become the 'store value'. Then from its political perspective, by redefining money through this idea of guarantee and, precisely, the origin of which he would envision in the law: that meant that money would become a political subject matter. However, it will be preferable to speak here of 'institution' and even 'national' institution, because this idea of guarantee carried with it the idea of a double assignment entrusted to the State to provide a guarantee of money and contracts. Locke would explain it very well, in what would be his main argument in favour of maintaining the par.

> The reason why denomination should not be changed is this: because the publick authority is guarantee for the performance of all legal contracts.
>
> (FC-9)

Since Locke spoke of the State in this way, that he entrusted it with an obligation, illustrates that he was talking about an institution, and he did so as a political philosopher. It is from this angle that it should be presented.

4.4 The problem raised by difficulties of interpretation

However, there will be some difficulties in demonstrating that and that refers back to the limits of Locke's interpretation.

1. First of all, there is a difficulty of method, which will impact the presentation of his views. Since, as is also known, the vast majority of his readers have had the surprising approach of crediting a metallist conception of money to him, contrary to his views. With regard to such a subject matter, this could only place them in an open-ended mismatch with the author they were trying to explain. Therefore, a systematic presentation of Locke's views will be required, as in the preceding chapters. Only the most representative divergences in understanding will be highlighted.

However, this would not exhaust the debate on the subject.

2. For the question that arises here is also one of a political choice – the par of the money – but a choice so strong that it affected the State's missions. The challenge of the interpretation has also been to understand its characteristics, even beyond the theories that have been attributed to Locke. However, the fact is that while some observers have ignored these issues – Hekscher in particular – a number of authors have taken a clear position on them, and not without gaining a certain amount of influence.

Alas, these authors have often been underrating Locke – especially on the subject of speculation – and were extremely critical, blaming him for an economic recession that followed the reform. The words that were used, moreover, were valid for any presentation: '[he] caused a drastic deflation'(Vickers), 'it was a social crime' (Fay), '[he judged] against the nation'(Steuart, Marx), etc... It has become very common today to judge Locke's thinking in this disgraced way.

Such a situation is, nonetheless, problematic. Not that the debate on this recession should be refused – it did happen really. But the problem is to recognise that it was about a financial decision – not just monetary one – that was taken from an institutional perspective, and the experience proved to be beneficial for the country. Yet, to have ignored these points – as these authors did – could only blur the understanding of Locke, including his political philosophy. This is how any criticism of Locke will be dealt with.

However, conversely, this will affect the approach to be followed in the second part of this work. This calls for a tiered approach on the subject of money, by discerning two separate discussions cross-cutting and including his 'Further Considerations':

- An in-depth reproduction of this conception of money that is so important to Locke's thinking, and which will be addressed in a systematic way (Chapter 5).
- On the other hand, Chapter 6 will take the form of a debate with the authors mentioned above, where the challenge will be both to reproduce Locke's institutional standpoint and determine the economic consequences of this famous debate on the money's par.

This will be carried out under the following heading:

Comment on bimetallism. It is important to note, for the rest of this work, that this debate took place at the start of concerns on the gold/silver exchange rate that would lead to the substitution of silver by gold as mentioned in the box above. Conceptually, this did not affect Locke's standpoint as the two metals had for him the *same conventional* status: silver would be the reference pledge, while gold '[if species are] at the weight... the law requires...will find [its] price'.[9] Nevertheless, this has not been the case for those interpretations which attempted to substitute the speculative context presented above with an economic analysis of the change in this exchange rate – which Locke would be accused of having underestimated. It will be demonstrated, however, that there were here a kind of theoretical illusion due to the obscuring of the notion of the store value of money.

This is where it will start.

Notes

1 The export of silver was estimated at more than 1 million for the period 1693/1694.

2 These figures depended on the gold/silver price.

3 M. Li, '*The great recoinage of 1696 to 1699*', 1963. See also Kelly, Op.cit., pp. 55-67.

4 Op. cit., p. 123.

5 'The severity of the penalties indicates that [monetary] offences are no longer tolerated' in '*Les fondements monétaires de la révolution financière*', 2007, p. 23–24.

6 Op. cit., pp. 145–152; see also Caffentzis, Op. cit., p. 43.

7 Eight experts would be invited, overwhelmingly favourable to the reform (Horsefield). According to Kelly, they would be divided on the question of the pair to a line opposing the 'intellectuals' – Wren, Newton and Wallis – and the 'financiers' in favour of Locke – Heathcote and Houblon. In fact, the latter were leaders or relatives of the Bank of England. Others like Hill, Child and Davenant intervened by themselves – the last two rather in favour of Locke.

8 Exactly from 5s 2p, to 6s 5p an ounce of silver. On the discussions that led to this report, see Kelly and Kleer ('*The ruin of their Diana*', 2004).

9 Letter to Clarke (Op. cit., 17/02/96).

5 Money, pledge and Natural Right

The purpose of this chapter is to restore Locke's conception of money and to offer a fresh reading of it, focused on the idea of a *national* money and related to *credit*. Since today, there is an inadequate interpretation in explaining its financial issue and the link to the decisions taken during the 1695/96 Monetary Reform. The aim of this work is, therefore, to explain these points.

This insufficiency, however, is no coincidence.

5.1 Locke's innovative status of metal and of money

It is due to the inability of imagining the *intellectual effort* Locke had to put into devising such measures, and in particular, the scope of this guarantee on metal which makes up the core. Since as is now known, the purpose of this guarantee was to defend the store value of money. Now if the idea appears simple to a modern mind, it was not so at that time – it was above all inaccessible from a theoretical point of view. It came up against this kind of intellectual barrier in the form of the material vision of money, which only saw metal and money as marketable commodities: they were seen from a circulation perspective, never from a lending perspective.

This was the case, of course, with the metallist school. Paradoxically, however, the same was true of the 'cartalists' that Locke would oppose in this monetary reform. For if the money lost its status as a commodity for these authors, it kept it as a circulation medium and metal still remained a commodity:

'Gold and silver', says Barbon, 'are commodities as well as lead and iron' (Op. cit., p. 7).

It is indeed *metal* that was at the heart of the discussions.

This aporia, consequently, should be located at the origin of Locke's view of money. Since whatever some readers may have said – Schumpeter in particular – Locke's texts would be unambiguous. They would all defend this breakaway idea: that gold and silver were not the marketable commodities that they were said to be, but *store values*. Locke spoke about their intrinsic value, making it clear: 'there is no such intrinsic value in commodities' (SC-66). It could not be clearer.

Nonetheless, probably the most important point here is not in the immediate meaning of this idea, however innovative it may have been, or perhaps not only that. It is in the *method* that Locke set in motion, the thought process and its affinity with his own tradition. For here too, the texts are unambiguous: it was in terms of Natural Right that Locke broached this question, and he never deviated from it. Consequently, this passage from the *Considerations* known as his fundamental position[1] should be quoted again – his full position is provided below. It is unequivocal:

> Mankind, have made [of metals] by general consent the common pledges.
>
> (SC-31)

Locke's use of the terms 'pledge' or 'general consent' has, therefore, a specific meaning. First of all, it means that the pledge status he gave to metal referred to accepted practices at the time, which bore witness to a financial use of metal: it was an 'arbitration tool'. However, above all, it means that Locke made it a *norm*, that is to say, a principle that redefined metal, and did so through its *store value function*.

Consequently, Locke's concept of money should be approached from this point of view: *it was a question of redefining the status of metal, of doing so in financial terms and of revaluing the role of money accordingly*. It has already been acknowledged that the monetary reform was the accomplishment of this.

5.1.1 The status of money

However, clarification is needed when confronted with such innovation and which concerns the as yet undetermined status of money. Since while it is true that Locke did *redefine* metal money, he did so without mentioning money, or at least explicitly: it does not appear in the quotation provided. Even if he did not mix up the two notions, there is still an ambiguity, at least at this stage of the presentation.

This needs to be explained.

It is argued here, however, that this standpoint can be clarified through the debate on money that has already been mentioned and that Locke conducted from within jusnaturalism. Since in reality, this debate had been initiated on a specific topic – the regulation of the land market. Yet, as is already known, Locke responded by referring to savings and the store value function of metal. This was also the thrust of his debate with Petty.

However, a step back is needed here from this, and a reference to Marx will provide that.

Indeed, this author revealed seeing money as a market commodity, like Locke's critics, had ramifications on maintaining the idea of *heterogeneity* for goods and markets.[2] This included, of course, the specificity of the land market. Now this is what changes with Locke and definitively. Since from the very moment he presented metal as a store value, it became the 'common equivalent', used for all goods, including land. He standardised everything. This is the meaning the author would like to give to this sentence placed at the heart of his theory of property, and which has been identified as referring to his definition of pledge:

It is the consent of the men who put the value on the gold.

(TGC-§46,47)

Since, taken in this context, it had a twofold purpose: (1) to bestow a natural character – in the sense of the State of Nature – to this pledge of metal, which would become a *global market broker*, and (2) to *replicate* from the money perspective the distinction between the two states of society. This meant that money would become a guarantee for metal, but a *political* guarantee and one that would have to be regulated.

Such is Locke's status of money, which explains both its national and financial dimensions – national because it became a market *unification tool* and financial through *the pledge status* allocated to metal.

However, if this is true, then a specific approach will be needed to demonstrate it and justify the conceptual innovation bestowed upon Locke. Though this is a serious assertion, and at odds with the current interpretation, it further suggests that Locke had both an institutional and a financial approach to money. It will, therefore, have to be defended on its merits.

However, the best way to do this is to reproduce the *critical* dimension that Locke was able to give to 'his' money. Indeed, the most significant aspect of this initial discussion is perhaps less the direct meaning of the term 'money' than the thought *movement* that conceived it, it is the fact that by approaching these notions Locke came up against and even revoked one vision of the economy, and the best way to illustrate this is to start from the debates he led on these subjects. Consequently, that is what will follow.

The purpose of this chapter is mainly to answer the two questions that govern Locke's meaning of money: that of the conventional pledge (paragraph 5.1) and that of the status of money (paragraphs 5.2 and 5.3). Quite logically, the latter will be addressed through his debate with

Pufendorf, his main jusnaturalist counterpart. However, regarding the former, which is undoubtedly the most sensitive, it can only be addressed from the only debate he had on this subject, his well-known controversy with Lowndes ('Further Considerations'). Admittedly, it will not be a question of determining the whole text, as it is still too premature, but of inquiring about the *method* he used. Since this will govern his conception of money.

This will now be addressed.

5.2 From trade practices to conventional pledge

The 'Further Considerations' were drawn up at the request of Lord High Chancellor Somers to oppose the proposed Treasury call for an increase in the par value of money. Due to this somewhat odd context, Locke compiled them into two clearly designated parts: (1) a *fundamental* part where he justified his standpoint. This will be discussed in Chapter 6, together with his economic case which, in fact, was autonomous (FC, pp. 47–55), and (2) a *critical* part where he simply responded to Lowndes' claims outlined in the box below (FC, pp. 24–109).

It is this second part that needs to be reproduced, bearing in mind that the heart of the debate has not been about inflation – as was stated – but about *speculation* and the link with the phenomenon of *overpricing of* 'bullion' which had recently emerged.

The Lowndes report is a technical report on coinage that will include 9 arguments for raising the par of money. Of the nine, only the first two will be outlined and discussed in substance (Op. cit., pp. 68–83), (SC, pp. 24–64).

It is due to the weakness of Lowndes' macroeconomics who would ignore price evolutions in case of raising the par. Hence, Locke will address this dimension from his own views, being content to answer the third (economic) argument of Lowndes (Op. cit., pp. 83–84) through a mere reductio ad absurdum (FC, pp. 61–78) – see hereafter.[3]

4 to 9 are technical arguments and will just be commented rapidly (Op. cit., pp. 84–91), (FC, pp. 78–109). There is little interest here. Notice only that Locke used the 7th argument on dishoarding to clarify his standpoint on the conditions of the Reform – evocated Chapter 6.

This was no coincidence. Since this overpricing signalled that arbitrage had become *standard practice* and the question arose as to what was at stake. However, the two dimensions should be distinguished apart: (1) the direct *cause of this overpricing*, about which the two authors debated, Locke seeing it in the loss of a coin's substance; and (2) *its level*, which referred to complex speculation on gold,[4] but which the two authors barely mentioned. They were reproached for this, but forgetting the fact that the decision at stake was all about silver coins.

However, this point should be put into perspective, as it does not weigh on the *methodological issues* of this debate. These will be pivotal.

5.2.1 Lowndes' theoretical analysis

Indeed, the question that arose here was to interpret a difference in value between two silver supports – species and bullion – and this necessarily referred to their store value. At the time, however, such concepts were poorly mastered, which means that these phenomena could only be interpreted through functions related to money circulation. This led to glaring contradictions, such as the more elaborated metallist theories, which implied that bullion should be... below the par value.[5] Consequently, this debate should be interpreted as an attempt to overcome these difficulties.

Yet this was an unsuccessful attempt by Lowndes. For his fundamental theory would be to set independent values for each support, which was, of course, paradoxical. Besides, today there is still some difficulty in understanding these assumptions, some seeing them as opportunistic inference linked to political games (Kleer[6]). However, in reality – and even if he was sometimes rough – there was a real coherence in Lowndes' analysis which converged with cartalism, and his standpoint should be interpreted as a reflection of their weaknesses. Since it consisted in explaining this discount solely by the function of money circulation and the idea of *its extrinsic* value. His text mentions an 'extrinsic value of silver in the coin' (Op. cit., p. 68); but it also means that he did not know how to theorise differences in quality of species.

With that proviso, his standpoint was expressed by this twofold idea:

1. That market metal was only a commodity, subject only to market fluctuations, in this case a greater scarcity in England, mainly due to the war:

> [B]ecause the Price of Standard Silver in Bullion is risen (from divers necessary and unnecessary Causes)…to Six Shillings Five Pence an ounce.
>
> (Op. cit., p. 68)

2. While species had their value from legal tender. Barbon, who supported Lowndes, appears to express the latter's standpoint better:

> Tis the PA upon metals that makes it money…by the authority of government did made current and lawfull money.
>
> (Op. cit., pp. 25,28)

On this basis, Lowndes' theory explained (1) that the overpricing of bullion was a market phenomenon which explained what he called 'a temptation' (Op. cit., p. 70), read: to melt down common coins in order to obtain the market price. It was therefore necessary to oppose it; (2) but it could be done – this was the important point – by realigning the par on commercial silver, *without any risk of movements* in other prices. He said, in response to Locke (FC-46): 'we need only to consider the… price silver bears in England [and that it will not]…decline' (Op. cit., pp. 77,78).

These are the ideas that must be linked to Lowndes, whose rationale was that the country would gain first by eliminating motives for speculation and second by more attractive coinage.

So, this was from an optimistic point of view.

5.2.2 Locke's response: starting with commercial practices

However, in reality, it was an illusion, perceptible once 'outside' of his theoretical reasoning while examining the specific conditions of this 'temptation': it occurred that for Lowndes, coins of different weights would have had the same value in metal once melted down. It was obviously impossible and Locke's response is then easily perceivable – thus emphasising the rationale behind his criticism: speculation as described by Lowndes did not exist, which made his theory on upward adjustment groundless:

> [A]n ounce of silver will always be of equal value to an ounce of silver: nor can it ever rise, or fall, in respect of itself.
>
> (FC-27)

Nonetheless, what needs to be understood – because this is the essential point – is the *method* that he would adopt and that would lead to his conception of pledge. Since, far too often, Locke's standpoint has been interpreted from a theoretical point of view, as if he had put forward an 'alternative theory' to that of Lowndes' (Dang[7]) or as if he had looked for an alternative analysis of the level of the discount (Kleer). This is a mistake. For Locke was content to oppose Lowndes with *the facts* – namely, describing widely known practices – this being his leitmotif to refute the latter's standpoint.

- This is, first of all, the case in his own analysis of speculation (FC, pp. 34, 39), where he emphasised that, apart from an anecdotal case, the only way to melt coins for profit was to relate it to international trade: the core of his argument being to show the arbitrage logic of the money changers – 'They, who…furnish [trade] with bills'.

  [A]s soon as there began to be a distinction between clipt and unclipt money…bullion rose [and] coin…will be melted down

  (FC-35,36)

- This is also the case for his first counter-argument (FC, pp. 26–61), where he was satisfied in challenging Lowndes' thesis, pointing out the behaviour of brokers. They discount, he recalled, only poor quality coins, making the 'temptation' as imagined by Lowndes impossible:

  Can it be supposed that a goldsmith will give one ounce and a quarter of coined silver [in milled money] for one ounce of bullion?

  (FC-26)

- But this was still the case for his second counter-argument (FC, pp. 61–64) in which he contested the new attractiveness of coinage, showing that the money changers would have even more margin to counter it (here in case of a trade deficit):

  [T]he goldsmiths and returners of money will give more for bullion to export, than the mint can give for it to coin; and so none of that will come to the mint.

  (FC-62)

These three arguments were, in fact, enough to answer Lowndes and can only be accepted.

- However, this was still the case with his discussion on prices, where he described the arbitrage practices of merchants between good and bad money,[8] or even here in this description which he said he inherited from practitioners (see Chapter 6 on these points):

Everyone selling their commodities so as to amends the number of light pieces for what they want in weight.

(FC-51)

It would take too long to outline all the examples provided by Locke. For, although they met different arguments, they were, in fact, all based on the same idea that was at the heart of lending activity: that metal had, in commercial transactions, the function of a store of value, which explained its arbitration role. As such, that was enough to counter Lowndes's thesis, paving the way for his own position.

This will be addressed however only in Chapter 6.

Since the question being asked here is upstream of this discussion. It is about this 'conventional pledge' which underpinned the status of metal money for Locke, and even further, his concept of money. It is acknowledged, however, that this status referred to the passage of the first 'Considerations' presented in the introduction (SC, pp. 31–33), and the comparison with this debate will be most helpful.

5.2.3 From commercial practices to the definition of pledge

Thus, if this text is re-examined henceforth, it will be seen that Locke mentioned this notion of pledge *in the same terms* as those of this debate: starting with practices 'in the field' which highlighted the store of value of metal, then generalising them through a norm enabling a genuine innovation to take shape. See below the quote in full, this is now the core of his thinking:

For Mankind, having consented to put an imaginary Value upon Gold and Silver by reason of their Durableness, Scarcity, and not being…Counterfeited, have made them by general consent the common Pledges…For they having as Money no other Value, but as Pledges.

(SC-31)

Locke puts forward here four ideas that will define his vision of metal.

(1) He first states that a *particular value* has been conferred on metal by the protagonists themselves ('*mankind*'), and he will qualify this value as 'imaginary', which at that time was clearly different from the traditional valuation of goods. He says 'having no other value but…'.

(2) He also states the reasons for these practices, and they will be vital. By speaking of 'longevity' and 'reliability', Locke is pointing quite clearly to a 'store function'. It was, therefore, a matter of asserting that the

protagonists mobilised this value in their arbitrations, as was seen against Lowndes: this being then confused with their 'imaginary' valuation.

But, making it clear that this is still only an empirical description, and this appears to be the key point.

(3) For Locke will not be satisfied with this description, and will point out 'in addition' that there was *acquiesence* on this fact, using the term 'consent'. He will even quote it twice, and this could only be a *normative approach* where this consent referred to an intellectual act aimed at generalising a practice. This was observed in the debates on interest. Above all, however, it was a binding act: this generalisation becoming a *reference point* in reasoning, including for the commercial exchanges – on which his opponents often relied.

(4) That is why he will talk about a *new status* for metal, which then becomes this famous pledge. This means that, because of this very norm, metals would be given special qualities, derived, of course, from the valuation presented above, but which would henceforth be *inherent*: those relating to pledges, thus conferring on them the two functions of money. It will, therefore, be because of their *very nature* – and no longer simply because of inter-subjective valuations – that metals would play this role in transactions.

Such is the meaning of this convention on pledge.

This is not a straightforward viewpoint, as can be acknowledged. Yet it is unambiguous. Above all, it leads to a conceptual innovation, namely, the introduction of a new element into the body of theory, designed to rethink money: this pledge status, or more precisely, this store of value function that *requalified* metals as pledges. Proof that Locke was aware of this latest development, he was prudent in clarifying his standpoint on two points: (1) by requalifying the 'imaginary' value of metals which would become 'intrinsic', which at that time meant value linked to a tangible essence:

> [T]he intrinsick Value regarded in these Metals…is nothing but the quantity which Men…receive of them.
>
> (SC-31)

This has already been mentioned in the introduction.

(2) Then factually describing the guarantee of value that was linked to this new status: this is the meaning of the expression '*are assured* to receive':

> [W]hereby Men are assured, in Exchange for them to receive equally valuable things to those they parted with for any quantity of these Metals.
>
> (SC-32)

It will therefore be concluded that this description summed up his standpoint on monetary metal:

> ==> And that this was, of course, a conceptual innovation: that of a conventional pledge that would be linked to money.

These points should, therefore, be read as the core of Locke's monetary thinking – his main theoretical breakthrough. They can now be considered as demonstrated.

5.2.4 The aporias of interpreting pledge

It is highly deplorable therefore that Locke's readers all shared a common attitude which can only be described as a denial of this innovation. The wording is not too strong, alas and no doubt it is due to this rejection of the normative approach which characterises Locke's interpretation.

For the fact is easily verifiable that almost all of interpretations missed this *status* that was given to metal, sometimes ignoring even the term 'pledge' used by Locke (Hekscher, Eich). By just focusing on the most sophisticated interpretations, they can be divided between those who rejected the scope of the convention, like Carey – see hereafter:[9] this amounts to seeing Locke as a metallist; and those who placed pledge *and* money under this convention, like Diatkine, or even Caffentzis:[10] which amounts to losing the status of metal. It is precisely here *the origin* of this uneasiness in interpretation – mentioned at the outset of this work. The truth is – that surprising as it may seem – the word 'metal' for Locke is still not understood.

Reference must be made, however, to the two most influential authors who are emblematic of this attitude.

1. Appleby was the first commentator though to have underlined the innovative dimension of money for Locke. However, she did so in such a restrictive way that she only retained the idea of an 'imaginary' value attributed to metal, which is right but stops when broaching its normative status. It is striking in this commentary on the passage quoted above:

    > [For Locke], the imaginary value upon gold and silver…had created the possibility of money exchange.
    >
    > (Op. cit., p. 49)[11]

It shows that at the very moment where she appeared to mention Locke's original position, Appleby was in fact denying the pledge status of metal: the consequences of this will be discussed in Chapter 6.

2. Then Schumpeter, who is one of the few economists to have recognised Locke's theme of the convention though. However, he thought he could conceal it, or more precisely re-interpret it by comparing this convention to a market valuation mechanism. He has been followed in this by Kelly:

> [At Locke] the monetary commodity acquires a 'price' through the market mechanism…[which] may be said to arise from 'consent'.
>
> (Op. cit., p. 291)

However, this is a contradiction in terms, which was tantamount to obliterating any reference to store of value, since a market only values the exchange value of an asset. That is why he re-attributed the metallist paradigm to Locke (Op. cit., p. 407). It would be an exaggeration, however, to speak of an 'error' for these authors, since this is only a problem of *method* – but with disastrous consequences.

Rejection has now been justified.

5.2.5 *Innovative uses of monetary pledge*

However, the most serious thing about such attitudes is not that they have missed this conventional pledge. After all, it is only a concept. It is that the consequences in terms of use, which Locke introduced as a possibility, have been ignored. It is worth emphasising this point, because it is the use of money that gives it its effectiveness. So, apart from the practice of saving, which will be covered with Pufendorf, there were two major consequences out of this innovation, which concerned both the *use of the pledge* and of the money linked to this pledge (this link will be explained in paragraph 5.3).

1. Regarding the transactions themselves, since Locke's innovation attempted to overcome the difficulties of mainstream thinking and its focus on money circulation alone.

Therefore, he would argue that the *actual* use of metal and money *differed* from that suggested by this model and already encompassed its function of store of value. He would therefore say that any transaction took place *for* metal – read: *to keep* the metal – while the commodity sold was only consumed. This skewness then constituted the basis for a new way of looking at the use of money:

> Silver…is the thing bargained for, as well as the measure of the bargain.
>
> (FC-4)

This has already been discussed in Chapter 1.

Yet in doing so, he was taking a resolute standpoint which merits a reaction. Since in reality, he was redesigning a transaction model that was already familiar – that of *payment* – as used in the lending model. He gave it a universal reach, and this could not fail to have consequences for the status of money. It was given a role akin to the one *it played in lending* and which shed light in advance on its political status: that of a guarantee of value.

So, here is a major sequel to this innovation.

2. However, this is not enough. It would be forgetting this other effect, which was the result of his normative approach and which can only be described as *ontological*. It may be useful here to draw a parallel with the notion of space in physics.

Since the fact of setting a norm has a particular scope when it comes to a field such as economics. Firstly, this means specifying a quantifiable object – metal – though not alone, but to make it the first element of a reasoning. It will logically precede the other elements. However, it means also that this object will determine the others, since it is the main one. It will then become a potential measure of economic goods and a measure that is notably homogeneous, the comparison with space[12] being here.

In doing so, above all, this represented a genuine conceptual shift, since the famous 'general equivalent' as theorised by Marx was set down here, namely, the object by which all other goods were to be measured…

> Being equated to [general equivalent]…the value of every commodity is…expressed as that which is common to all commodities.
>
> (Op. cit., p. 44)[13]

The foundations were thus laid not only for a new use for the pledge, that of measurement, but also for a new entirely quantified reasoning, which invalidated the previous ones.

That is why Locke was extremely precise. First of all in his 'Considerations', insisting on the general measurement role played by money, as was seen in his market analysis. He was equally so in his criticism of Lowndes, which was ultimately based on this principle of quantification. This was precisely so, finally, in his 'Further Considerations', where he made this equivalence the *only theoretical proposal* of his analysis, and on which his entire standpoint would be based. It needs to be quoted, even repeated again because it is the first sentence of this text:

> Silver is the measure of commerce by its quantity which is the measure also of its intrinsic value.
>
> (FC-1)

It must be interpreted in two ways, which will form the main result of this chapter. It is both:

• The starting point of his theoretical vision, already pointing towards the determination of the money's par value. In Chapter 6, it will be seen that all the positions he assumed on this occasion will be deduced from this idea of measure.

• But it is also the conclusion of the whole movement of thought which has just been reproduced. *A movement, in short:*

> ==> *that relied on the practices of economic players to lay down not only a status, that of a pledge, but two new functions for metal and money: payment (and lending support), and measurement.* This completes the presentation of the conventional pledge.

However, such a result, while it helps to understand the pledge of money, cannot by itself explain the very notion of money. It would have even contributed to rekindling queries on the matter.

5.2.6 Concerning the property theory

For as was often outlined in this work, this 'equivalence' function that has just been pointed out was an important issue, particularly from a jusnaturalist point of view: it referred to the debate on the extension of the market. The fact that it is to be found here means that a pivotal idea is alluded to, linking two dimensions of Locke's thinking, the philosophical statement and the economic approach. The question of consequences naturally arises, in particular, the political and even philosophical principles that enabled it.

They certainly will help in determining the status of money.

However, for this, there is only one possible step, even if it breaks the unity of the explanation. It means starting again from this jusnaturalist debate on money and from the response that the final argument of Locke's theory of property comprises. This is the topic of the second part.

5.3 Locke and Pufendorf: money and the land capital market

Indeed, it seems difficult to access the full meaning of Locke's concept of money, without referring to his well-known 'theory of property', or without reading it in light of the debate he conducted on the subject from within his own thought tradition: a debate with Grotius and especially Pufendorf,[14] but excluding the School of Salamanca.[15]

However, to understand his approach, the start must be from this idea that the regulating principle of these debates was to *maintain* the thesis of Aquinus, for whom the *measurement function* linked to money was of conventional origin. The question being asked was about metal: because it had been thought of in a restrictive way by Aquinus, as if it was economically offset by coinage – as was seen in Chapter 1.

It can be imagined, therefore, that this standpoint had become incompatible with trading practices. This debate should then be seen as a re-appropriation of this theme of measurement, but within the framework of the actual use of metal. This was already Locke's realm.

As for the views of the three authors, they are as follows:

- First of all, Grotius should be mentioned as he would put forward the idea that metal was an *independent* measure of values, and that it was so through its market value. This was an advance in relation to Aquinus, which took into account fluctuations in the value of metals and, more generally, the reality of international trade:

  All that is used to be the measure of other things must be…invariable…and among the things that can be estimated are gold, silver…
                                                                      (Op. cit., II, XII, XVII)

However, the price to pay was the ambiguity of the theme of *convention*. From the point of view of junaturalism, this left the analysis incomplete.

5.3.1 Pufendorf and the regulation of the land market

- This explains the prominence of Pufendorf, who chronologically followed Grotius, and would reconstitute this theme of convention.

Nonetheless, he would do so around three ideas that were probably at the origin of Locke's thinking:

(1) that money was a political tool, which also means that it was *external to the State of Nature*,[16] but whose function of measurement was the result of the willpower of Nations. It was therefore the result of a convention:

> [T]he most civilized nations by agreement thought fit to set a certain eminent price upon some particular thing as a measure for the price of everything.
>
> (Op. cit., LV, ChI, §XII, p. 467)

(2) but – and this is the key point – this convention would not only affect money. It would also affect the metal whose qualities endowed it with this measurement function. Pufendorf meaning here, its own measurability and, above all, its scarcity – read: fluctuations in the quantity of metal:

> However, this use of [moneyed-metal[17]] does not follow the nature of things but the common consent or agreement of Men.
>
> (Op. cit., p. 467)

This was, therefore, exceeding Aquinus' approach, since the theme of conventional measurement was being referred to, but by giving the metal this economic dimension that the former refused. Indeed, this theme of scarcity made it possible to translate the mechanism of domestic prices within a country, as well as a changing value of metal linked to its international aspect – metal, according to Pufendorf 'should have the value of many things'. The recent influx of metals into Europe was a case in point.[18]

(3) In doing so, Pufendorf introduced, however, a certain duality between money and metal, which under Natural Law obtained the same status, while remaining bearers of potentially different values. This is why he put forward the idea of a possible regulation of money by fixing its par value.

> ==> It was the combination of these three ideas that formed his theory of money.

This standpoint was, therefore, quite sophisticated, which explained its impact. Notably, it had the advantage of bestowing metal with a nature that was both economically independent and conventional for the first time in this tradition. However, it had certain limitations. Since besides the ambiguity of this subject of regulation – whose origins go back to Aquinus – it only recognised a single economic dimension of the metal, its scarcity. It was, therefore, only able to delineate market phenomena, but not financial issues such as credit and/or the value of assets.

This explains how Pufendorf approached the theme of regulation because one of his major objectives would be to describe the influence of money itself on the economy. But, this description would partly be a concern around the values linked to both land and land economy – his theory being that the market was often encouraging irrational behaviour such as, for example, punishing too good a harvest by a collapse in prices.

That is why his viewpoint would enable money to be regulated in accordance with this land economy, the idea being to seek a form of stability. This proposal should then be interpreted as his main conclusion. It can even be seen as pre-empting the well-known 'landed interest':

> It is evident that in fixing the price of money the greatest regard ought to be at land.
>
> (Op. cit., p. 470)

This, more importantly, also reintroduces Locke's answer, and the debate opened at the end of the first chapter is now rekindled.

5.3.2 Locke's criticism of Pufendorf – store of value and State of Nature

It is indeed striking, when comparing the two authors, to see how close their approach to money was. Thus, the theory of property recaptured those same themes of money, the two states of society,[19] including this convention on metal which they alone advocated. Consequently, they both shared a common framework, but which also enables the *critical approach* that Locke adopted in response to Pufendorf to be identified.

To do this, and following our first discussion presented in Chapter 1, the well-known argument on money must be re-examined, but now including that it falls under the State of Nature. Locke is unambiguous on his point, and through this remark, it can be observed that two *conceptual changes* encompass the essence of his concept of money. (1) Locke first borrowed the convention on metal from Pufendorf, but 'lowered' it to the level of this State of Nature, and thus to the level of transactions between individuals. Men would give consent and no longer Nations…

[S]ince Gold and Silver being little useful to the Life…has its value only from the consent of Men.

(TCG-§50)

(2) …to explain, but it has already been pointed out, that this convention would be based on a status of pledge. This justified assigning it a store of value capacity.

This is clearly an approach similar to his criticism of Lowndes, but in a different *philosophical* context. Since it was a question here not only of the empirical use of money, but of its *legitimacy,* and this would have a twofold meaning, with immense ramifications.

• This, first of all, meant that this store capacity *legitimised* innovative uses and in particular, what has been called the dynamic of savings which, just as a reminder, was based on the store of value function of money.
• This was, thus, the third innovative use allowed by the pledge status bestowed on metal. Nonetheless, this status would here have this essential effect of allowing its reallocation for the acquisition of land which Locke would justify through a specific argument – related to 'wastage'– which is presented hereafter.[20] This latter discussion, however, would go beyond the scope of this work. Locke states precisely:

[T]he invention of money gave…the opportunity to enlarge possessions.

(TCG-§48)

It can therefore be deduced – which confirms the hypothesis raised in Chapter 1 – that one of the challenges of Locke's theory of property was to affirm the legitimacy of this idea of financial savings, and a market logic for land. This argument will, of course, be compared with the debate with Petty in Chapter 3. It was indeed the same idea, except that the point of view expressed here was a moral one: and that consequently the first criterion was *justice.*

• That is why Locke would conclude, in what would become the final phase of his argument:
  • By first explaining that this 'new' use of money could be a factor of inequality in 'proportion', he said, 'to different degrees of industry' (TCG-§48);
  • That it was nonetheless morally justified. Since it emanated from a convention which, as will be remembered, is a *norm* here. This

is why he focused on this idea, which concluded his debate with Pufendorf, but also marked the accomplishment of his theory of property:

[A] tacit and voluntary consent…[on] metalls…found a way how a man <u>fairly</u> possess more land than he can use.

(TCG-§50)

The thesis is clear, but the stakes were high: it means that Locke argued *as legitimate the idea of a market for land, including the logic of extension of property*, and that he indeed based it on the affirmation of a conventional pledge. This is how it will be remembered in any case.

It is an understatement, therefore, to say that we have reached a key point in his thinking, which necessarily calls for reflection on the debates that have taken place on this subject. However, it will be dealt with at the end of this chapter, so as not to deviate from the purpose here, which is the status of money.

This can, henceforward, be achieved in-depth, again in stark contrast to Pufendorf.

5.3.3 Political society and the national status of money

Indeed, the latter had a *twofold* understanding of money, where money and metal were under the same – political – state of the community. Though this is what changes with Locke, and even resolutely, since the convention, which had become natural, now only concerned *metal*. This inevitably changed the status of money, which became *relative* (to the metal-pledge): but not in the sense that it would be merged with it, but that it would *remain* a political topic from then dependent on this metal.

Here again the texts are very clear.

- On the one hand, because Locke showed the existence of specific uses for money, which necessarily characterised it: he stated that it was used like a 'token', that metal could not be – a 'token' at that time meant an instrument of account. This point will be developed in detail in Chapter 6 to address some of the criticism of Locke.
- However, especially because the two objects would refer to two different perimeters which would distinguish them apart: the pledge convention being universal – read: international – 'mankind' consents to it. This is not the same case with money, which only ever appears national, as was underlined by Eich.[21] Locke never diverged on these two points:

[T]he use of…money, is, that every man in the country, where it is current…be assured what quantity of silver he…contracts for.

(FC-7)

This could only mean one thing: that of duplicating through money the duality between the State of Nature and political society, and thus making money the political counterparty of metal. Such is the logical effect of this debate with Pufendorf: to introduce a duality between money and pledge:

> ==> The former becoming the *national or political* support of a conventional and *natural* pledge. Obviously a comparison will be made with his credit analysis.

Achieving such an outcome, however, shows that the foundation of Locke's concept of money has been attained, and *found in this duality*. So, it is useful here to step back and complete this debate.

5.4 Money as an institution

Indeed, the question that was asked in this chapter was about the meaning of the concept of money in Locke's work. However, it was asked in a specific context, that of the 1695/1696 monetary reform and the measures taken under his influence. This inevitably raises the question of the relationship between the two.

Since it must be seen that this reference to Natural Right provides the answer to this question. For two reasons:

1. For an *epistemological* one first of all, which refers to the dimension of *abstraction* that appears here for money. This dimension is now immediate, since the fact of distinguishing between pledge and money literally compels such an epistemology. This helps to illustrate the discussion already held on the subject in Chapter 1. However, it must be pointed out because of the debate on interpretation that took place on this subject.

It should be noted incidentally that this *abstraction* of money topic has recently been raised by several commentators, often philosophers, generally to contest that Locke was a metallist (Caffentzis). This can be accepted. Nevertheless, so far this has been done only from Locke's philosophy of knowledge, arguing that moral notions were defined there as abstract notions.[22] So, it was only natural that the same should be true of money. Garo, who was very precise, stated that:

> Locke considers money as a mixed mode, it is its own archetype and can be defined by pure convention.
>
> (Op. cit., p. 21)

However, the limits of these interpretations must be deplored because they went no further than the epistemology of money. Thus, stating *politically* that money was an abstraction was first to make it a political *object*, since it was henceforth stripped of all material reality: it therefore became the 'object' of a monetary policy and, thus, necessarily *national*. However, it was above all to convert it into a *project*, and even an institutional project because of its novelty. In the end, it was merged with the rules that had to be established.

2. Though also for *a philosophical reason* and this is the final outcome of this debate – because this project was determined solely by its relationship with the pledge. Yet this type of determination is not new as was seen with regard to interest.

That Locke referred to it for money would therefore have this meaning:

> ==> That if the pledge were a norm, it would provide the natural framework in a jusnaturalist sense which the 'monetary laws' had to respect: these laws referring here to the management policies implemented through his political action.

It can, therefore, be said that they complete the definition of his conception of money.

Hence, all that has to be done now is to translate this idea into practical consequences, which can be done in three points:

1. This would first confirm the political nature of money at a decisive moment for the English community, a moment when the idea of a national money itself was being questioned. The term 'political' should therefore be interpreted in the way that Locke always meant it: where *the use* of money was not only a matter of *law*, but also of *its sovereignty*. However, that also meant that this theme of law included the theme of *sanctions*. This is indeed a known characteristic of Locke's thought (TCG-§125), but which has the stronger meaning here of justifying the policy of control which was followed since the reform of 1695/1696.

It must be recognised then that his 'Further Considerations' could plainly handle this type of position: from its plea to reactivate old sanctions against 'money clipping' to this proposal for action against the use of clipped coins. He has been sufficiently criticised for this:[23]

> In England everyone may not only refuse any money bearing the publick stamp if it be clipped … but he that offers it in payments is (passible) to indictment.
>
> (FC-8)

2. On condition though to specify that this 'sovereignty' was not free in the way it is commonly understood, where a State would issue 'its' own money unconstrained. On the contrary, it was determined by this pledge norm which it had to respect. It was therefore, to paraphrase Dunn, *limited sovereignty*.

Yet applied to this subject matter, this could only mean one thing: that at the same time as the state regulated the use of money, it *had to commit* it to this norm – in this case, to guarantee its metal composition. This is why Locke would always associate this guarantee to the notion of uses of money, as here he describes the sign on the coin 'as it were a publick voucher…of such a weight' (FC-5), or again here: 'money' becoming before our eyes a legal instrument guaranteeing the pledge:

> [T]he end of the publick Stamp is only to be a guard and voucher of the quantity of Silver which Men contract for.
>
> (FC-8)

==> So, too much emphasis has been placed on these points, not acknowledging here the major political measure of the 1695/1696 Reform.

3. However, in doing so – and this will be the last point – Locke bestowed money with the same qualities that he recognised in the pledge and, in particular, that store of value, so central to this discussion. In any case, he did so nationally, where it would become this lending instrument and this equivalence tool that was already the pledge. Hence, this quotation, so important in the 'Considerations' will be a synthesis of this discussion:

Now Money is necessary to all these sorts of Men, as serving both for Counters (read: in a national area-CR) and for Pledges, and so carrying with it even Reckoning, and Security.

(SC-31)

It completes the presentation of the concept of money for Locke, and just to sum up, it could be stated that for Locke:

==> 'money' was an institutional project, rooted in Natural Right, which was both a support and a guarantee of a conventional metallic pledge - the stakes being to confer money with innovative functions: equivalence, and savings and lending support.

The meaning of the concept of money for Locke is now definitively explained. It should be remembered that this concept was put into practice during the monetary reform of 1695/1696. At least, that is what this discussion has shown.

5.4.1 Still a partial outcome

However, if this is the case, and at the very moment it is reached, this outcome requires further analysis. Because it raises the question *of the monetary policy associated* with these measures: and, in particular, this famous question of par value which was at stake in his debate with Lowndes. Since it was this par, in practice, that bestowed on money its effectiveness.

It is, therefore, necessary to go back over this debate.

This is, nonetheless, a very specific issue – explicitly linked to the relation between money and credit – but one that has given rise to too many criticism against Locke to be dealt superficially. It can only be approached from its historical context. Therefore, a mid-term conclusion will be used to present it.

5.5 Towards the par debate

The thesis behind this debate is that the monetary reform that Locke spearheaded – and because the issue also concerned the credit system – was a decisive moment in the financial revolution. Retrospectively, this is why it can be referred to as an institutional approach, because an innovative management principle had been put in place. It would be long-lasting – the famous 'gold standard' – synonymous with the stability of English money. It was this principle that would then transfer this *reliability* to the English financial system.

==> Without envisaging it as the only underlying factor, it can be said that this success was mainly due to the monetary reform.

So, if the criticism levelled at Locke must truthfully be broached, then the impetus bestowed on lending through this new money – for which he must be credited – must be assessed. Without going into detail, as this is not the purpose here, it refers to these points:

- To the *growth in lending*. (1) With a huge increase in sovereign debt, which increased from £3.3 million in 1692 to £14.2 million in 1700 – a proportion that was only reached during the great wars; (2) as North explains, it is this increase which will facilitate the appearance of private credit structures, notably through its floating part (the famous 'tallies'):

> [A] stable market for public debt provided a large and positive externality for private debt.
>
> (Op. cit., p. 825)

(3) Thus, if there is a lack of data to measure private credit, there will be indirect evidence of it with the emergence of a genuine capital market – visible as early as 1700.[24] See Carruthers on this point.

- Next to the impact on the *different banking models*, with (1) the stabilisation of the Bank of England, which took place to the detriment of the deposit banks (see Chapter 6). 2/ but also the failure of the Land Bank, nonetheless supported by the King and given power by Parliament at the beginning of 1696.
- This failure would be a hard blow, with a margin call of less than 1% for its capital raising in June 1696. Hence, if some readers preferred to envisage conjunctural reasons, like Rubini,[25] it must first be perceived as an example of a change in investor opinion, arbitrating from then on in the national money (read: debts based on this money):

> [At the] date of 1 August…only £7,100 (out of 1,250,000) was subscribed and only a quarter of that had been paid in.
>
> (Op. cit., p. 709)

These points could surely draw to an end the intention of this work since they are sufficient to reveal *Locke's decisive contribution to the 'financial revolution', one and a half years after the creation of the Bank of England, three years after his address to the English Parliament.* In a way, there should be nothing further to add.

However, this judgement should still be deferred.

5.5.1 Economic recession and criticism of Locke

Unfortunately, even though this type of image may have been conveyed by, for example, Macaulay, it is no longer in this way that Locke's contribution is elucidated. Reference is made here to those commentators presented at the end of the last chapter. It can even be stated that interpretation has become more and more malicious over time. It would differ from this presentation on two points.

1.   First of all, the financial issues that have been mentioned should be disregarded, as they can be deemed to be *outside* the issues of the monetary reform. In other words, this reform is today considered as 'purely monetary'. Yet, this is clearly a mistake.
2.   The economic difficulties which followed the Reform are undeniably the main focus of attention, which were incidentally incontestable, but which would be used in a real case against Locke. They are usually presented in terms of these three points: (1) a sudden shortage of money followed immediately after the implementation of the Reform (May 1696), and which generated an acute financing crisis, especially for the State: the symbol of this being the peak in the discount rate of the tallies – above -30% in the summer of 1696;[26] (2) this shortage led to an economic recession, with the typical phenomenon of non-stop disruption in the payment chain – and particularly, according to Kelly:

> Rents remained unpaid, debts unsettled and people were reduced to extending indefinite credit.
>
> (Op. cit., p. 64)

It would be accompanied by phenomena of impoverishment. (3) Finally, several authors speak about a deflation phenomenon (Vickers), which is much more debatable. In any case, the seriousness of the recession is confirmed by the appearance of reported social unrest in certain cities, including by Macaulay.[27]

It was these events that are at the heart of the case against Locke, since he is accused of having refused the increase proposed by Lowndes, which is said to have *cushioned* the negative effects of the Reform. Furthermore, even accusing Locke of having kindled this refusal out of *ideology*: which means that not only were his views unrealistic, but *de facto* served private interests. Here Steuart can be quoted, he who set the tone for such interpretations (his thesis being that Locke would have sided with the 'young banking industry'[28] *against* the national interest):

> Though Mr Locke felt that...creditors...must lose... by Mr Lowndes's scheme, yet he did not perceive (which is very wonderful) that the debtors...must gain.
>
> (Op. cit., p. 555)

It should be underlined that this thesis is economically weak. This will be dealt with below. However, it is not the most important point. What is important is that behind the economic criticism, even the political dimension of Locke's thought has been targeted and that, moreover, he was denied any concern for the common interest. This was the case for almost all Keynesian and Marxist authors.

> Such allegations cannot, however, be accepted. As it has been observed throughout this debate, Locke's approach was philosophical, and it is not possible to take a standpoint at such a level without wanting to transcend any private interests. It can, therefore, be presumed that Locke was given a bad trial.

Anyhow, the best way forward from now on is to judge the facts, and thus resume this debate with Lowndes, as only the criticism aspect has been identified. This will be covered under the following observation.

Concluding observation: the meaning of the argument about money in theory of property

It is beyond the scope of this work to determine the full meaning of the theory of property. It would include too many dimensions – especially legal ones – which would extend its breadth. It can be argued, however, that it is possible to single out the crucial section on the argument about money, thus concluding this theory. This has given rise to meticulous discussions, mainly on its *moral* status – its relationship with the State of Nature – however, the limits of which could be justified as *conceptual*. Since most of them are based on the misunderstanding around the difference Locke made between 'metal money' and 'money'. These discussions are as follows.

For a long time this theory was interpreted from an institutional perspective, as a theory defending in *principle* the right to property. It will predominantly be a utilitarian interpretation, but also Sieyes, in France, can also be cited, with the known outcome.[29] It could be called a lasting consensus on the subject. Nevertheless, this interpretation was *simplistic*, and this point is today acknowledged because it was limited to the ethical and legal aspects of the text, without any real reference to the economy (Tully). That is why the discussion revolved around Macpherson's 'individualist' interpretation, who was the first to insist on this monetary argument: his thesis being that Locke's objective was to establish, still under State of Nature, the *principle* of capital accumulation - which included the wage relation.

This thesis drew attention and is still being defended. Yet its weakness is that it concealed the theme of the convention on metal: since for Macpherson, Locke was a 'metallist' who reduced money to gold like a *commodity*, and he interpreted his theory by assigning it only with the paradigm of exchange.[30]

It would, therefore, in turn be contested, but based on a poorly mastered method. Since, if this conventional dimension was evoked, it would be to argue that it was about *money* – and not metal. That is why it would be deduced that this convention in Locke's position referred to the Political society: the idea often put forward, being that it was part of the founding contract of Political society. To cite Tully:

> [M]en [enter] a state of…convetousness…by consenting to the introduction of money:..Locke's analysis furnishes the motive for entering the political society.
>
> (Op. cit., p. 150)

This is why – and while there is *no argument to justify* it in the text – this argument around money is today read through a certain tension between State of Nature and political society, with two interpretive axes that correspond to the two positions (moral and social) presented in Chapter 2:

1. For the first axis, this theme of the convention would induce the idea of a market dynamic, *politically regulated via money*, and the purpose of the theory would be to justify it – which amounted to attributing to him Pufendorf's thesis. This standpoint would be that of the most well-known authors, with two lines of interpretation:
   - (1) Tully's hypothesis, which interpreted this regulation as a land redistribution policy; and
   - (2) Ashcraft's hypothesis which was that Locke described a monetary policy of economic growth:

[M]oney is…an instrument for the development of trade.

(Op. cit., p. 277)

2. Many authors, however, went even further, often referring to the argument by which Locke justifies the inequality of ownership: their hypothesis being that he would describe a logic of *disruption* of the State of Nature through market.

- (3) A majority, including most economists, seeing it as a conflict of interests between owners and non-owners (Chevallier, Polin [1960], even Appleby), or between rich and poor (Vaughn)…

[W]hich is usually described as a conflict between 'haves' and 'have nots'.[31]

…where that institution of money would have a stabilising effect.

- (4) The thesis of Caffentzis should also be mentioned, where he sought to base this conflict of interests on the notion of monetary accumulation, which was mentioned in Chapter 1, and leading him to put money at the heart of the social contract:

For Locke, civil government has its origin and end in the regulation of money.

(Op. cit., p. 21)

The spectrum could seem wide and contributes to a certain sense of powerlessness of interpretation. Yet in reality, it is narrow since the logic of all these authors has been to reduce the scope of the State of Nature, and therefore to weaken the moral significance that Locke gave to his theory – in other words, by substituting it with a sociopolitical bias. This was remarkable for Caffentzis. This is why it is argued here that this problem of interpretation should be resolved as soon as Locke's 'natural' status of the convention is re-established, together with the fact that it *only concerns metal*. The outcome is then quite simply:

==> that the theory of property had this purpose of legitimising both the idea of a market for land and the market practices that concerned it. This can be summed up by talking of a capitalisation impetus linked to savings.

This is, in any case, what can be deduced from this chapter on money.

It should, however, be underlined that this does not amount to rehabilitating Macpherson's theory – beyond his reference to the State of Nature. Since his argument went beyond the idea of market, to address the *very principle* of capital accumulation. This explains, in particular, his insistence on Locke's theory of credit, which he interpreted as a justification of the advanced (contractual) forms of accumulation. He was very clear on this point:

> Locke can assume that neither money nor contracts owe their validity to the state…it is the postulate of moral reasonableness of men by nature.
>
> (Op. cit., p. 210)

So, it is clear from Chapter 2 that this is not the case since, if for Locke the use of the pledge in credit is natural, its *contractual nature* makes it a matter for the political society: it is *regulated by law*. There is no reason why it should not be the same for the *salaried work*.

==> It was, therefore, wrong to interpret Locke through the Marxist prism, as a proponent of the deregulated accumulation of capital.

However, if this is the case, then the question of the political output for this theory remains to be addressed. Since historically this is the way it has been approached. The answer, however, is less obvious because it cannot be summed up in a 'positive law' proposal – which has traditionally been done when talking about the Right to Property. It referred rather to a number of possible State courses of action – as long as Locke clearly identified them. However, here again the reference to money could help us. Since, as has been observed in this chapter, its role as a market *operator* was inseparable from its institutional dimension: which means that it would become a *State Institution* (and not its essence as Caffentzis believed). Under these conditions, Locke's political action would have replaced the silence of the Treatise.

Therefore, the last stage of this work will broach this institutional concern.

Notes

1 For the status of this passage, see the bibliographical note.
2 'We have, on the whole, nothing but fragmentary equivalent forms [of value], each excluding the others', in *Capital*, 1887, p. 43.

3 Lowndes states only: '*money will acquire more goods or pay more debts*', Op. cit., p. 77). Hence, there was no reason to limit the increase to the 20% proposed, why not even more? This would be Locke's response.

4 The mechanism involved the purchase of goods in England, resold for gold abroad, and then resold for goods or silver in England. The golden guinea will thus increase from 21s – its base price – to 22 then 30s in 1695, then 22s (April 1696).

5 See Chapter 1: the reason was that, for theses authors, the value of money was due to its *use* in the market...what a bullion couldn't have. This contradiction explains Appleby's surprising silence on this point.

6 According to Kleer, through Lowndes' report, the Treasury wanted to build a political alliance with some bankers who financed it, often members of Parliament (Op. cit., pp. 545–550). There is no proof of that.

7 '*[For Locke] knowledge of the causes of variation in the value of money was very important*', Op. cit., p. 768. See also Ormazabal [2007].

8 '*Any merchant...shall sell it for a...less number of shillings...to anyone who will contract to pay him in milled money*' (*FC-26*).

9 Carey will see the weight of the metal, at Locke, as an '*objective standard of value*' ('*Locke's philosophy of money*', p. 60). This is correct, but insufficient. For metal remains an economic good in this case, and Carey will refuse the idea of a 'social convention' that would make it a pledge (in '*Locke's Species...*', p. 11). He would pay for this mistake by not understanding the status of measure of the metal (see Chapter 6).

10 On the consequences of this confusion, see below our concluding remark.

11 Compare Appleby's expression '*possibility of money exchange*' with Locke's text which she claimed to explain, but which states '*Men are assured*': the notion of store of value has disappeared.

12 For Locke like for Newton, space is a *form* – the same as Kant – but real. It would therefore function as an *a priori* by which all objects could be measured (Essay-LII-ChXIII).

13 Among Locke's contemporaries, only Vaughan managed to accomplish this idea, which is not surprising: '*[by analogy with geometry], money is [the] third line by which all things are made egal*', Op. cit., p. 3.

14 Grotius, *Le droit de la guerre et de la paix-FFT-1999*; Pufendorf, *On the law of Nature and Nations*, 1721.

15 Namely Suarez and Molina. That Locke ignored this school has been noted by many historians.

16 There are differences between the conceptions of the State of Nature for Locke and Pufendorf, but they are less important here. Since what counts is the movement of thought accomplished by Locke.

17 This term is borrowed from the translation by Barbeyrac, who distinguishes here between '*argent et "monnoie"*'. Rightly so, it seems.

18 '*According to the calculation of...Bodin...everything must be worth ten times as much today, because of the abundance of Gold*', Op. cit., p. 470.

19 Pufendorf's civil society corresponds to Locke's political society.

20 The argument is that by selling a surplus on the market, there is no wastage of products that could not have been consumed otherwise.

21 Op. cit., pp. 24–28. It is all the more regrettable that Eich did not understand the financial perspective of 'Locke's concept of money.

22 ' *The mind...can put...simple ideas together in several compositions and so make variety of complex ideas without examining whether they exist'* (Essay...-LII-Ch22-§2).

23 Horsefield attributes Locke for wanting to rehabilitate 'measures dating back to Elizabeth 1' (Op. cit., p. 59). This is forgetting that the legal framework was different: traditional coinage considered species as private commodities certified by the State. This was no longer the case for Locke.

24 Diatkine (Op. cit.) speaks, at that time, about the creation of a hundred companies.

25 Rubini attributes this failure to management errors on the part of the project holders: *'relatively slight changes often determine success'* – in *'Politics and the battle of the banks'*, 1970, p. 710. The argument does not seem to be in keeping with the failure. If this were the case, other 'better tailored' projects would necessarily have emerged.

26 Bank bills were discounted at -24% beginning 1697. For Macaulay, the recovery was significative late 1696, for Dicskon, from April 1697, but very rapid.

27 Op. cit., p. 706.

28 In *'An inquiry into principles of political economy'*, 1767. That Locke sided this 'banking industry' could be accepted, if it was not for Steuart's idea that Locke had acted against the national interest.

29 French declaration says: *'Le but de toute association politique est la conservation des droits naturels...Ces droits sont la liberté, la propriété...'*.

30 To be precise, Macpherson used the term convention, but from a 'Schumpeterian' perspective that misrepresented its significance: *'Money, Locke emphasizes, is a commodity'*, Op. cit., p. 206.

31 Bouillot (Op. cit., p. 14).

6 The par value and the monetary and financial system

It is generally considered that the debate between Locke and Lowndes determined the last stage of the monetary reform: where the decision to recall the species was taken implicitly, but where the question was raised for a possible increase in the par. The rate was even fixed at around 20%, and it was Locke's intervention that allowed it to be refused. That is why, it is generally considered that Locke's response to Lowndes – which only took up a part of the 'Further considerations' – contained the essence of his standpoint.

This is, however, a superficial vision, which neglects the fact that Lowndes' theories were too limited for this debate, mainly confined to a focus on speculation. It was, in fact, a monetary analysis that did allow no access to the financial issues of a potential decision, and it is this point which is still badly understood.

Since this decision to maintain the par was not purely monetary, as is too often thought. It was a global choice which concerned all the country's contracts and fixed income, and the reason is that the metal value of these items was directly dependent on the par of the money. They were denominated in *numerary* – read: unit of account – but payable in species:

> Altering the Standard, will defraud the King, the Church, the Universities...Hospitals.
>
> (FC-12)

The same was true, above all, for the banking sector, whose assets were related to similar issues. Therefore, such a choice had the effect of repositioning the financial sector as such in relation to money also determining its relationship with the State. So, it is first in this way, which is of an *institutional nature*, that Locke's main argument against increasing the par of money should be perceived:

The reason why denomination should not be changed is this: because the public authority is guarantee for the performance of all legal contracts.

(FC-9)

This argument must, indeed, be taken literally. Since while it disclosed the recommended level for coinage, it first and foremost revealed a State's mission – a mission that had been inadequately fulfilled up until then. It is consequently with that in mind that Locke's standpoint should be approached:

> ==> It was, in fact, a matter of deciding not only State action on money, but also on a future monetary and financial system.

Thus, it is from this point of view that his criticism of Lowndes must be judged: although essential for his readers, they were of *secondary* importance in his reasoning.

Consequently, this is a highly regrettable attitude to interpretation, by which such events are often reproduced, as it depicts them based only on Locke's criticism of Lowndes. Since an institutional approach – whatever its purpose – is a *principled* approach and can only be driven by the idea of *general interest*. By nature, that could only be Locke's.

However, the misrepresented way in which his economic views have been described was incompatible with this point of view. It could only limit its issues, reducing them to a simple monetary approach and through that to the defence of individual interests. It explains, in any case, this surprising attitude, which consisted of attributing Locke with patterns of thought that he did not have – the patterns of liberal authors – in order to better assign him with a specific ideological point of view. Hereafter, the two schools of thought that dominate this subject are the following:

- The Keynesian school represented here by Appleby and who accused Locke of having anticipated monetary liberalism and being hostile to the State;
- And of course, the Marxist school, for whom Locke only defended the interests of the 'rising bourgeoisie', often associated with the 'interests of owners'.

It is these preconceptions that are contested here. Since in reality, these have led to the philosopher being analysed, not for his own views, but from pure hypothesis on his intentions. His text, however, is unequivocal, and it will be shown here that he had both an institutional and financial standpoint, always focused on the general interest. He did so first, as was just observed, by raising the issue of the State's guarantee as a political agenda for both money and contracts. Moreover, he applied the same approach to the economic issue, where he took into account the risks of a recession instead of hiding them. His position being, besides, almost a condensed version of this discussion: it consisted of linking the economic evaluation of contracts with the recurrent problem of speculation.

The question being, therefore, to know whether this was justified.

Consequently, this presentation will follow a specific way. It will be necessary, actually, to resume the analysis of the 'Further Considerations', which started in Chapter 5, but by restoring now Locke's fundamental standpoints: on the par value of money (paragraph 6.1), as well as his economic arguments on the risk of recession (paragraph 6.2). However, rather than giving a direct account of them – as they are now at hand – they will be broached through a critical discussion, responding step by step to these two channels of interpretation. It will be seen, indeed, that far from countering Locke's positions, they will re-establish its legitimacy.

First of all, what could be the most contentious approach regarding this work.

6.1 The monetary foundation of the financial system

Locke's most frequent criticism in the 20th century could be described as Keynesian – despite his silence – because it was inspired by his criticism of monetary liberalism. It was conducted by a series of authors close to Letwin; according to whom, Locke would have anticipated on the liberals' refusal for State monetary intervention. However, it was, above all, based on the work of two, Vickers and Appleby, who assimilated Locke's point of view to a deflationary standpoint, comparable to certain liberal positions of the 1930s.

The important point, nevertheless, for these authors is more specific. It is that Locke had defended these positions out of *theoretical weakness*, precisely because of a limited conception of money: this would have prevented him from considering State action. This is why they ignored Locke's explicit political standpoint and just looked at this 'guilty' conception, trying to deconstruct it and reveal its logic. That is the reason why they restated the importance of the *numerary* dimension in *monetary policy* issues. Not without reason, moreover, because it is always at this level that these policies are envisioned, following the example of legal tender.

Yet, Locke – and this is the core of the criticism – would have failed to identify this dimension. This was apparent in his analysis of everyday transactions, where he would have failed to recognise the specific role of this *numerary*. Appleby stated that he confused money with metal,[1] Vickers too

> Locke failed to see that…money…even clipped…was…accepted at face value…the effect of Locke's position would be engender a monetary deflation.
>
> (Op. cit., pp. 70,71)

This was where the criticism transformed into judgement.

For Locke would be accused of being blind to this issue as well as the real price-setting mechanism. In other words, he would not have understood that a money even clipped had a proper value, which would allow to 'stabilise prices' and that, furthermore, a 'raised' money would have had the same effect. Hence, this blindness would be responsible for the post-Reformation 'deflation'.

The criticism is harsh, but defended and echoed by a whole school of economists who would see in it a retrospective disapproval of the gold standard. Hence, Fay, see below. However, it went well beyond economics. As by speaking about hostility towards the State action, it attained, in fact, the thinking of a philosopher who was implicitly accused of ignoring the institutional dimension of money. This is why it calls for a comprehensive response, including a return to Locke's concept of money, which will enable us to clarify this dimension.

6.1.1 The dimension of numerary and monetary policy

First of all, it is about this epistemological issue related to numerary which is crucial for this debate.

- Since if it is true that Locke rejected the idea of a value linked to numerary – which would have been an 'extrinsic value' – it is simply wrong to accuse him of having ignored its independence. This point has, moreover, been emphasised by several authors, including Carey, and reference can be made to their comments.[2] However, proof of this can be seen in his discussion with Lowndes and, in particular, the arbitration examples that he mentioned.

As in this discussion, Locke clearly pointed to the case of everyday transactions, mentioned by Vickers. He explained in detail the use of 'face value' money which then answers the core of the accusation:[3]

For who will not receive clip'd money whilst he sees the great receipt of Exchequer admits it and the bank and goldsmith.

(FC-97)

His standpoint is also easier to understand in terms of method and evokes his analysis of banking behaviour. This is a *normative* approach that distinguishes between what would be a natural price (Smith) measured in *metal* and the *difference* with it, necessarily expressed in numerary and due here to the disruptive role played by the Treasury. Such a gap could even be described as a 'rent'[4] in the sense of the classical economy because what is described here is the effect of a *subsidy* for using money and not proof of a value attached to this 'numerary'. This aspect will be broached in the second paragraph.

- However, not investigating further would be falling short of the problem posed, which concerned the status of monetary *policy*. Therefore, there may be some consensus with Appleby and Vickers at least on this point: it is true that at that time there was a problem of understanding this status of numerary. This was especially the case for metallists, who saw it only as a measure of the value of metal, like in coinage, and therefore could not imagine such policies.

So, questioning Locke was not so unjustified.

Nevertheless, what must be understood – and there the debate on concept of money will be resumed (in Chapter 5 – paragraph 5.3) – is that *he too* had identified this difficulty. Since, for him, it was the *metal* that assumed this function of measurement, and this necessarily endowed numerary with the independence that it would have in modern thought. Locke was always very clear about that, pinpointing it as a specific function of money:

[O]ur coin being that which Englishmen reckon by.

(SC-66,67)

It must, therefore, be concluded that he fully understood the *epistemology* of monetary policy, and this is essential, even though it may appear a 'technical' point.

6.1.2 The core of Locke's position

For as was stated in the introduction, Locke's objective in this debate was, above all, the monetary guarantee of contracts. It was thus inevitably a question of comparing these objects – denominated in numerary – to money. Now, what has just been demonstrated is that he knew how to conceive this comparison when it posed a problem for mainstream thinking. Thus, both Vickers and Appleby were answered...

> ==> that they simply confused Locke's conception of money with that of metallism and thereby *missed its political dimension*.

So, if this point is accepted, then the political core of Locke's standpoint can be reached. This will be henceforward surprisingly easy. Since, it would simply consist of expressing the recommended value of contracts while presenting it as an objective: the State *had* to guarantee it. So, the important point will be *his defence*, the reasons he put forward.

This is, in fact, the meaning of the first part of 'Further Considerations' which will set forth two principles (FC, pp. 1–25).

6.1.3 The two principles of the 'Further Considerations'

1. Locke would first reaffirm the measurement function of money, and he would do so in a normative way. This point has now been identified and revisits the conventional status of metal pledge. He just has to be quoted...

Silver is the Instrument and Measure of Commerce... The intrinsick value of Silver consider'd as Money, is that estimate which common consent has placed on it.

(FC-1)

...but also commented on. For the fundamental aspect here is epistemological; and again the comparison should be made with physics.[5] It is precisely therein that this measurement by metal is relative and not absolute – as Carey thought – and this relativity clarifies strongly its political dimension.

Since 'relative measurement', in pure logic, means that it is defined as a unit of measurement – here the quantity of metal – whose standard would be conventional and not natural as it was previously. This standard would, of course, be the par value of money. However, this conventional nature would, above all, have two effects on prices and contracts: (1) the nominal price of goods would change *directly* in relation to the par value, which was contrary to the current position, as was seen with Davenant. Market prices would, therefore, also be *relative*, which would be the very heart of Locke's economic argument:

Commodities (as is natural) shall be raised in proportion to the lessening of the Money.

(FC-48)

(2) Yet if prices were relative, this was not the case for *contracts* whose value was determined by the par: they were absolute. This is a key factor as it would mean that the choice of the standard would become a *political act*, and even a major act because it determined these values.[6] Locke's theory prompting the following statement:

==> that the context – namely, the existence of *already signed* contracts – determined both its meaning and fairness.

A fairness which meant, it seems obvious, leaving the par unchanged.

2. This is why the second stage of the argument would be conclusive, and it would be so through this affirmation of a State's *duty* in guaranteeing contracts. The idea was already included in his first 'Considerations', but it is a fundamental issue here:

The stamp, [and] the denomination...together give...the publick faith as a security that money contracted shall be as such value.

(SC-146)

Since in advocating such a duty, Locke was certainly defining the par value of money, but, above all, he was defining the relationship that money should have to the financial world. He thus shaped a monetary and financial framework, as well as the rules to be followed by the State, and this can only be described as *institutional:*

==> that entailed *laying the foundations* of a financial and monetary system. So, as can now be stated, this was the main objective of the 'Further Considerations'.

This is why, it is important here to take a step back in this respect.

6.1.4 *The moral foundations of the monetary and financial system*

As it is not possible to have an institutional view, whatever its purpose, without stating the *reasons* justifying it and which would thus become its true foundation. This is the very essence of an institution, and Locke did not fail to recognise this. However, two levels must be discerned here:

1. The very principle which justified this State action and which could only be in the general interest.

    ==> This is why Locke would make *collective faith* the goal of State policy, by making the guarantee it offered – on money and contracts – the means to achieve it.

It can even be said that this was the most important thesis of all his economic thinking.

2. And the considerations behind this decision which would become the philosopher's own *moral* reasons. Respectively…

    *   The defence of savings and the justice to which contract holders should be entitled: these two principles were merged together in what has already been quoted.

It will…destroy the public faith when all have trusted the public… shall be defrauded of 20 per cent of [their estate.].

    *   And the fight against *speculation* – see below – these four ideas summing up his fundamental standpoint. It can, therefore, be said that these reasons formed the core of Locke's position, the heart of the message that his 'Further Considerations' were addressed to the English Authorities. Since collectively,

    ==> they form a complete argument, which led the State – through the par value of money – to build what would be the first monetary and financial system of the modern era.

This should be seen as the main outcome of this first discussion.

However, it must be recalled that this was the last time Locke intervened in the financial revolution. It is, consequently, far from useless to recall the standpoint taken a few years earlier on the issue of banking regulation. For these are the *same themes* that he raises here – the same lending incentive and the same justice to which savers were entitled. There is even a stronger link between savings and the general interest because the State is endowed here with a specific mission. It must, therefore, be concluded that there was, during this revolution,

    ==> a certain unity in Locke's interventions characterised by the same principles including the state guarantee of money: the defence of savings and of its transformation through monetary and financial regulation.

In fact, the only topic which is practically absent here is *specula-tion*, which was central to the previous analysis. It has so far not been encountered. However, this should only be seen as an intended choice of presentation in order to empower the economic dimension of this debate. Since speculation will play the leading role.

6.1.5 The economic dimension of the monetary reform

So, the least that can be said is that the debate is now unavoidable.

Since, it has already been stated, it was in the name of economic criti-cism that the views just presented were concealed: the idea being that Locke refused political regulation, and plunged, therefore, his country into deflation. Yet, it has now become necessary to deal with this argu-ment. That is what will be done by asserting two points:

- That this problem of speculation not only *cleared* Locke of these accusations – paragraph 6.2.
- But, on the contrary, it shed light on the political issues surrounding his standpoint – paragraph 6.3.

However, caution should be applied about such a debate, particularly with regard to its methodological aspects. For a judgement of this nature cannot be made without a retrospective analysis of the economic situ-ation, and this raises the question of the concepts and theories adopted for this purpose. However, it is argued here that modern interpretation stumbled over this difficulty, and that, in reality, its criticism of Locke was merely the reflection of *an anachronic use* of its theoretical tools. This needs to be explained.

6.2 Contracts, hoarding and Locke's responsibility

It is generally accepted that the monetary reform was followed by major disruptions linked both to its implementation – as described in the box below – and to the significant decline in the stock of money circulating in the country. The figure of 25% – *but measured* in numerary – can be used for silver coins. The metal measure is evoked in the argument. It cannot be neglected, and it was on this basis that Locke was accused of unrealism. Since he would have acted at the wrong moment, dragging the country into serious deflation. It is even not uncommon to see comments reshaping Lowndes' standpoint in this way (Fay, Appleby).

- Technically, the Reform consisted in the Treasury's refusal to accept the wrong money on a fixed date – 4 May 1696 – forcing the taxpayer to recoin his coins to pay taxes. However, it came up against the weak coinage capacity of the State services.
- The months preceding the reform would be marked by the growing expectations of the protagonists regarding the following phenomena: (1) of flight from money which would be reflected in market prices, and (2) traffic of clipped coins.
- The less and averagely advantaged population[7] seemed to have been the victims. (3) Tensions that have arisen in some cities were proof of this. They would remain limited to the first months of the crisis.
- From May 1696, a 'cumulative bottleneck' appeared in the coinage services, with a prolonged and fairly massive freeze on money. This is the primary cause of the liquidity crisis mentioned in the text.

It took more than 12 months to solve this situation. From Kelly, Horsefield and Macaulay.

There are, however, two aspects in this standpoint, but the one concerning Lowndes will be discarded – as already mentioned above. On the contrary, the first aspect can be interpreted independently, and the following authors can be associated with it:[8] Fay, Appelby, Vickers, Hawtrey, Eltis, Hutchinson, even historians like Feavearyear and Li. In fact, it draws a comparison between Locke's action and the monetary crises experienced under the gold standard, which can be interpreted on the basis of inflation phenomena. The argument, therefore, followed the same pattern, explaining that this debate on the par followed a situation of inflation – due in particular to bank money issues – and that this situation would require a downward adjustment of the money. Locke, therefore, would have taken the wrong direction:

> The inflation of credit war nevertheless the immediate cause of that depreciation.[9]

In itself, this argument seems pure simplicity. However, it poses a methodological issue which actually makes it unsuitable for a debate of this kind – and it will only be covered indirectly. (1) On the one hand, it has not been validated through the reconstructed data, which did not indicate any significant medium-term movement in prices. Kleer's explanations are referred to here.[10] (2) Above all, however, it contained such a problematic bias regarding money that it blurred the terms of this debate. See the following description.

6.2.1 The monetary assumptions of the criticism against Locke

Indeed, it must be seen that this inflation thesis is only *theoretical* and its only meaning was to affirm that there would have been a reference value for money – called *the* value of money[11] – and that it could be compared to the movement of prices – and in this case judged to be overvalued. However, there is a tricky point. Since this assertion refers to a moment in time when there was competition between several monetary supports and, in particular, between numerary and metal. It presupposes, therefore, that a support was chosen for this 'value of money'.

Such a choice, however, seems impossible without contradiction because the only way to accomplish that would also be theoretical. It would be to rely solely on *numerary* - which was the 'language' of prices, so to speak – and to assign to it this reference value. That is why these accusations of deflation against Locke have always been consistent with this surprising position: that the main value of money was linked to certain uses of it, and referred to numerary 'instead of metal'. *Numerary would have had a value of its own.* It will, of course, be noted that this argument echoes the previous debate on transactions 'at face value'.

Fay can be quoted here, but also Appleby, Vickers and even Kelly:

> The detachment of the money of account from its old weight and fineness was something which Locke was not prepared to comprehend.
>
> (Op. cit., p. 149)

These statements are really astonishing and all the more so as *no author* of this time defended such positions.[12] Since one could tolerate that the pre-crisis years were thus interpreted with such a theoretical contrivance. However, what is being discussed here is the moment when arbitration had become the *norm* in practice, and it was achieved through metal: probably, furthermore, before the markets 'registered' it with the bullion overpricing and the decline of the pound. Of course, this does not mean that clipped money was no longer used, as was made out, but that it was rejected *as a measure* when the question arose. It was then up to the metal to act, and it did so because it *only* was accepted as a store of value. This is what Lord Houblon would officially reiterate at the heart of the crisis.[13]

However, if proof were still needed, it is to be found in speculation, which was the lifeblood of this crisis, in clipping and hoarding. Since what was trimming if not recognising the value reference bestowed on metal? What was hoarding if not stockpiling it? It is worth reaffirming the following data: out of 14 million silver coins in circulation, at least 5 were 'clipped' and another 5 were hoarded.

Yet, is a value of numerary mentioned? Which would be 'separate' from metal?

In fact, such an approach is an *anachronism*, which amounted here to denying the function of money as a store of value. Yet, not measuring it – as these authors did – led inevitably to distortions in interpreting this debate, namely, concealing the two distinctive dimensions of this function: (1) the financial dimension, as Kleer[14] underlined it, which overlaps with that of contracts (see also Wennerlind); (2) but also that of speculation, which would be minimised to harmless 'anticipations' on exchange rates[15] – and here Caffentzis'[16] criticism should be adhered to. This was particularly the case with gold, which is the subject of the observation below.

However, above all, this led to not discussing the positions really defended by Locke.

Remark on the gold issue: In relation to this monetary debate, Locke was accused of having underestimated the pressure on the gold/silver exchange rate which reappeared shortly after the monetary reform. Kelly speaks of a 'blind spot' in relation to a stance taken in 1698 for the board of trade.[17] However, this is only partly justified. On the one hand, it is true that Locke did not anticipate this phenomenon, which marked the beginning of the substitution of silver by gold. Yet, by blaming him here would mean confusing two aspects which must, on the contrary, be distinguished. (1) His institutional standpoint which affected silver, and whose deciding factors – for him as for the observers – would first of all be speculation, which is discussed here; (2) and a straightforward analysis of the exchange rate movements reactivated by that pressure on gold.

Locke's understanding suffered as a result.

6.2.2 A recession linked to the scarcity of money

For it must be added, and this is obviously crucial, that if Locke ignored those debates on inflation, he was, on the other hand, fully aware of the recession issue being raised. Adding, further, that he responded it based on these two dimensions that are contracts and speculation: his argument being that a conflict of interests between them weighed on the risks of recession. He announced this as soon as the dedication of the 'Further Considerations':

'It will deprive blameless men, of a fifth part of their estate…'. Locke speaks here of the contract holders, 'only to be bestowed on men growing exceedingly rich by publick authorities', and here of the speculators.

However, what has just been demonstrated is that this argument could only be ignored on the basis of these hypotheses about inflation and numerary value.

==> means that this was unsuitable for such a discussion.

This is why, according to the author, the only way to approach this question on recession is to do it using the *customary* terms of that time, and which emphasised the *scarcity* of money (read: by making it the sole explanatory factor of activity), but *while accepting* the reserve function of metal. From this point of view, the debate becomes clearer.

Since if the question asked is that of a decline in activity, then this amounts to (1) presenting an increase in the par as a contrivance designed to avoid it, what it meant for many observers – if not for Lowndes; and to (2) comparing two choices, which are documented below from Kelly (Op. cit., pp. 61–63): the idea being that, by making money scarce, Locke would have contributed to such a decline. Either, respectively,

- Lowndes' suggestion, which would have decreased the stock of silver coins from £14 million to £12.9 million, still measured in numerary; and
- Locke's suggestion, which decreased it to £10.3 million (the data for gold are 9.8, 8.9 and 7.6, respectively).[18]

In practice, however, this means evaluating Locke's standpoints because it was his opinion that was implemented, and not without grounds.

However, in order to do so, caution will be required with regard to the question of market prices. Since, in the case of an increase, a probable rise in these prices should have transpired, as the *metal content* of species would have decreased. Such a phenomenon was well known at the time[19] and anticipated by the majority of the group of experts (Horsefield). Of course, it weighed in Locke's favour. Nevertheless, an immediate increase could not be conceived either like Locke did with the idea of 'relative price', because of the well-known weak price-elasticity of the markets. That would, moreover, be his main weakness, and Kleer must also be followed on this point.

But, this was just a relative weakness.

6.2.3 Locke's position on the risk of recession

Since if the 'Further Considerations' are read in this way, they would be unambiguous and truly coherent. They would provide a three-point answer which could be presented in relation to the interpretations of Steaurt, Kleer and Kelly – likely the most precise ones.

1. Locke first warned – but was not followed – on the implementation of the Reform, arguing that there were risks of a bottleneck linked to coinage (Kelly). This is why he continual requested for transitional circulation 'at weight', his aim being to ensure the fluidity of money circulation:

    > If clip'd Money be call'd in all at once, and stop'd from passing by weight, I fear it will stop Trade.
    >
    > (FC-13)

Unfortunately, these obstacles did indeed occur, and even strongly as indicated in the box. Locke could not, however, be held responsible for this.

However, the important point is elsewhere, in the economic analysis itself.

2. Then, it is better to quote his argument directly, which was stated long before the reform and from which he would never deviate (Steuart, Kleer):

    > It will rob all Creditors…of their Debts, and all Landlords…of their quit Rents…without any advantage to the Debtor, or Farmer…
    >
    > (SO-4)

It should be interpreted under the hypothesis of an increase with a threefold meaning.

1. It first of all means that Locke made the guarantee on contracts the *criterion* behind his standpoint, condemning here the arbitrary reduction of the holders' assets ('to rob'). It is indisputable, since the financial world was already arbitrating 'in metal' and the decrease would have affected creditors 'cash', then depending on the movement of prices for lessors and other revenues.

This argument will, of course, be linked to his warning about investor confidence.

2. However, it also meant that the context prohibited the effects of positive wealth that would have 'compensated' these negative effects as Steuart suggested:

- Nor for the debtors, apparently winners, but who in reality had to refinance themselves at the *same* rate, no matter what. The argument, acceptable as predominant, refers to the following discussion concerning the Treasury:

> For he that takes up Money to pay his Debts, will receive this new Money, and pay it again at the same rate he received it, just as he does now [with] our present Coin.
>
> (FC-48)

- Nor for farmers whose economic equation would remain stable when measured in metal: an argument which was, however, debatable for the reasons outlined above (FC-50,51).

There would thus be a loss of wealth in this increase, potentially for savers and fixed income contracts.

3. Now this differential, and this is the second facet of the argument, would be absorbed by speculation (Kleer). Most importantly, it would be removed from the economic cycle, which affected the very heart of the 'increase thesis'. That referred to a *dead loss* in metal, where normally an increase should have been witnessed:

> [T]hose only who have great sums of weighty money…will get by it…which hoarding up of money…have no other merit…than prejudicing our trade.
>
> (FC-47)

It can be understood now that this was a warning in essence of the pending allegation of recession. In terms of principles, it concludes Locke's argument.

However, it needs to be completed with regard to one aspect, particularly in response to the ambiguity of his commentators on this subject.

6.2.4 Money hoarding at the centre of state financing

It is important to note that this 'hoarding' which was condemned by Locke did not refer to an extended activity – as other forms of speculation often did. It was a very well-placed activity, and essentially to be found in the financing of the State, because of the masses of money that were being collected, and because of the Treasury's 'tolerant' policy towards clipped money. This point was very widely known, at least among decision-makers. This is why the Goldsmiths and tax officers were often – and rightly – accused of it (Kleer).

However, it should also be argued that this concerned a major issue, both politically and in terms of the interests at stake.

It should, therefore, be pointed out that there was a basis for agreement between the two authors (Locke and Lowndes) – which Kleer was unable to see. It concerned both the nature of this speculation and the fact that the reliability of money would free up hoarded money.[20] It was hence used 'to cushion' the crisis.

On the other hand, and this is the last point, Locke was the only one to point out that an increase would result in an *additional gain* for these hoarders, and would be removed from circulation, at least initially: which is also hardly questionable, since the gain was automatic. He would even go so far as to evaluate it (the figures are underestimated compared to the reconstructed data):

> Money hoarded up...Lowndes computes as 1600000, so that there will 320000 pounds given [to hoarders].
>
> (FC-47)

It will then be his last argument against an increase of the par.

It is, consequently, deeply regrettable that so much has been neglected in interpretation, which was true of Steuart, just as much as those contemporaries being discussed here. Since everything indicates that this standpoint was not only coherent, as can now be discerned, but realistic. At least this is what emerges from Table 6.1, which specifies the movements affecting money over these years.

Table 6.1 Money circulation in England during the crisis years – from Kelly (Op. cit.)

Type of coins	06/1695	05/1696	12/1696	12/1698
Silver Money	14.1	14.1	10.9	9.5
• Clipped	5.1	5.1	2.5	– (+0.2)
• Hoarded	5.2	5.2	3.8	1.8
Gold money	9.4	9.0	7.1	7.7
• Hoarded	2.9	2.2	1.0	1.5

The table indicates in fact two things: (1) the importance of this 'hoarding', which must be understood henceforth as *the major issue* in this debate – with the melting down of coins. (2) But, it suggests also that it was *behaving as Locke indicated*, and this would be the conclusion of this discussion.

6.2.5 The economic significance of Locke's standpoint

Since, henceforward all the arguments to appreciate Locke's standpoint on this economic issue have been collated. If now they are taken globally, then three points can be made:

1. That a significant part of this recession – but an *unmeasurable part* – was inherent in the very choice of the reform and the conditions for its implementation. The risks were even partly anticipated (FC-dedication). But this is not the real issue in this debate.
2. As for judging on maintaining the par on activity, of which Locke was accused, the probable effects of an increase must be first examined, and include these three compensatory factors: (1) the effects on speculation, (2) the wealth effects linked to the par, negative in case of an increase, but also (3) the movement of prices over a longer term – see hereafter on external trade.[21] Unlike with the financial world, alas, there are not enough data to be able to judge this – but simply to point out that *ideas of size were comparable*. That was enough to dismiss the main points of the accusations.

For in reality, what this examination revealed is that we were at a time *when a downward adjustment in activity* was becoming inevitable – but where Locke's standpoint, like that of Lowndes, was in fact a matter of arbitrages which concerned both:

1. The specific interests, and it is clear that Locke made them focus (1) massively on speculation and to the benefit of savings, and also (2) on the institutions and protagonists which were the largest users of clipped money, that is, first and foremost, the Treasury and, incidentally, private individuals (probably numerous in the middle classes).[22] Locke explains this below.
2. In a particular way, Locke clearly opposed the long term to immediate concerns.

From this point of view, and whatever its apologetic character, Macaulay's quotation does not seem unjustified, which stated that:

England had suffered a terrible crisis...[but] which was succeeded...
by...prosperity.[23]

3. Since what must be understood, and this will be the final point, is
   that the ultimate issue in this debate was not monetary, as Locke's
   critics really yearned for, but *financial*. This was already the conclusion
   of the first discussion and simply reinforced here: it was in this *dele-
   terious effect* which would have caused a real loss on credit, in case of
   an increase. As it would have been engendered by a State that was still
   suspicious, but which would have arbitrated against its own savers, in
   favour of speculation.
   ==> Without too much emphasis, it could be stated that its legitimacy was really at stake. It is a misconception to believe that there
   would have been no economic effects.

Consequently, it is from this perspective that the criticism of Locke
should henceforth be answered: these critics not only exaggerated the
economic consequences of his standpoints, but also masked the political
and institutional stakes.

   ==> In fact, through a sort of theoretical bias, it was those who
   accused Locke of rejecting the State who actually ignored it.

In any case, this is the conclusion that will be drawn in this work.

6.2.6 State financing and conflicts of interest

...And if we stick to Locke's only explicit standpoint, then that should
be sufficient to finalise it. So, it would now be very easy to link it to the
financial revolution.

However, in reality, these results call for a last discussion, but one
that would focus more on Locke's action than on his thinking. This is
illustrated through the importance of the issue that has been mentioned
in the debate on speculation – the financing of the State. Since by taking
a strong stand on it, Locke took *de facto* standpoint on vested interests
which were at stake here – be they collective or individual. The scope
could, therefore, be called into question.

It would even be a mistake not to broach it.

6.3 Financing of the State and the issue of ownership

Since it gave rise to extremely severe criticism, in which Locke was
accused not only of having silenced these vested interests – which could

be accepted – but of having illegitimately served particular interests. While several authors have implicitly judged this to be the case, Marx will be cited here because he made this episode an emblematic example. This should have illustrated the 'class' point of view which Locke was said to have defended during these events.

But rather than provide a lengthy presentation, a quote from Marx will suffice here:[24]

> '…[T]he state gained considerably upon the score of taxes, as well as the creditors upon their capitals and interest; and the nation, which was the principal loser, was pleased, because their standard (the standard of their own value) 'was not debased'.

In fact, this argument followed on from Steuart's and should be interpreted as follows: it first referred to this Treasury policy that accepted bad money, but also pointed out the *discrepancy* that would be created by the reform between certain protagonists. Since it was in good money that the State would have to repay debts contracted in bad money, and it would have done so through taxation. It was these discrepancies that Locke would have encouraged – and Marx condemned him for it.

It has to be recognised, nevertheless, that the criticism was strong, even if it must be underlined that banking intermediation limited the gains. It was actually *rooted in facts*, since it is true that the reform protected the interests of the savers, who were the creditors of last resort. This was all the more serious because it referred to the theme of 'ideology' which would have underlain Locke's standpoint. Here again, the quotation from Marx speaks for itself:

> Locke who was an advocate of the new bourgeoisie in all forms, the manufacturers against the working class…the commercial class against the old fashioned usurers, the financial aristocracy against the state debtors, took up the challenge against Lowndes.
>
> (Op. cit., p. 93)

It was thus the heart of the philosopher's thinking that was being targeted since his connection to the general interest was refuted. Yet the aim of this work is precisely to counter such an idea. It can therefore only be finalised by answering this question.

This will be carried out in two parts: first, a methodological one where the link between lending and property will be mentioned, and then to the heart of the problem posed.

6.3.1 The unfeasibility of Marx's criticism

First, concerning the method, but it will be succinct. For Marx's theses are always very precise on this idea of interest. As is well known, they are aimed at *collective* interests which Locke would have defended by maintaining the par. Yet, these collective interests are synonymous with 'social classes', and are defined by their relationship with property. It is, moreover, this idea that will be restated when broaching the theory of property: Locke was again and again accused of defending the interests of the owners.

But while the position was clear, it was no less problematic when it came to lending. It even failed, and if necessary, the proof of this can be noticed in the surprising way Marx spoke of the 'State debtors'. For at the time, taxes were primarily levied on land which meant, if we follow Marx, that the adjustment due to the reform would have been partly based on the 'gentry'. So it is hard to see what 'class ideology' Locke was defending – this simple reminder illustrating the weakness of such accusation. For in reality the mechanisms that Marx denounces here, namely, the transfers linked to public lending, were unrelated to ownership. A *loan is in fact only a contract* relating to money and, thus, at the time, credit crossed almost all social groups, entrepreneurs as well as landlords and even bankers. So, there could be no social interest in this debate, in the way Marx meant anyway.

Consequently, the comment made to Ashcraft about saving needs to be restated.

> ==> If Locke took sides in this debate, it was not out of social interest, but out of morality.

And it were false to see it as unfavourable to the State, because Locke included the possibility of a compensation tax and the duty for citizens to subscribe to it – see the specifications hereafter.[25] This was still consistent with the general interest.

6.3.2 The realignment of State financing

This was not just about method, it was also empirically that Marx was vulnerable. Since his criticism was intended to be explicit, seeing a social advantage behind Locke's standpoint. But in reality, it inappropriately scaled down this standpoint. It limited it to precisely the analysis of single loans, where the only point in question was the balance of 'amounts lent and paid back'. Yet, on the contrary, it should be interpreted in a systemic way. Since this State financing was already a *global* reality at that time and where the problem for the State-debtor was both its *credit* and the *interest rate*.

It was with this in mind, moreover, that Locke had argued against the increase.

So, from this point of view, creditors and the Treasury could not be set against each other, as Marx did, and even condemn the losses for the Treasury. Since if there was a monetary reform effect, it was indeed in the 'signature' of the State that it would be seen and which would undergo a considerable recovery – due also to the support of the Bank of England, as is mentioned below. The following sequence illustrates this observation, which would successively witness (1) a severe crisis for the Treasury, linked to the shock of the Reform, as was stated in Chapter 5; (2) coupled with support from the Bank of England, with a new loan (£200,000) and above all the option of redeeming the tallies (end of 1696); and (3) then an increase in the same tallies: in less than two years, they went from a discounting of −36% (March 1697) to −15 (May 1698), then −6% (November 1698).[26] Where was the loss for the Nation?

Yet, this does not mean over-interpreting Locke by presenting it in this way. Since he had indeed defined this mechanism from the very beginning of the financial revolution:

> [W]ere the States…begin to pay their Debts, the Creditors, rather than take their Money out…would let it stay in, at lower Interest.
>
> (SC-111)

In fact, what this data suggests is the emergence of a new financing system, where moderate rates would be the trade-off of new guarantees provided to creditors – in other words, *where the latter's interests would be linked to those of the State*. Consequently, Marx has to be criticised in the same way as previous commentators, Steuart too:

> ==> *by scaling down Locke's standpoint to the short-term aspects only, he disregarded the issue of State financing.*

Thus, it is easy to see that the Monetary Reform made a major contribution to this.

However, extensive analysis is inevitably required here to provide a global answer, mentioning the *operators* behind this new means of financing, namely, the banks, and even the different banking models. So, the fact that the initial theme of this work will be covered is a strong indication of its culmination.

6.3.3 Towards the Bank of England institution

As has been pointed out from the very beginning of this work, this Reform came at a time of fierce competition between banking models. It was noted that it concerned in particular the State financing market. However, it is obvious that the choice of the money's par value meant taking side in this conflict of models. This can be identified from an examination of their situation – limited here to the two main ones.

1. The deposit banks, first of all, were the *losers* of this Reform. For while their credit position allowed them to make some gains on the Treasury, as Marx noted, they lost heavily and twice: firstly as speculators as was seen earlier and, secondly, as operators, above all, since their assets – in cash – were going to lose value in relation to their liabilities (read: in relation to the claims of their depositors). It was therefore the model itself that was affected.

That was enough to explain its future decline as acknowledged by all the historians.

2. But what the deposit lost, the credit that gained, and of course, the Bank of England had a predominant influence on this model. It gained mainly in *competitive positioning*. For as was shown from the beginning of the work, the Bank of England's model – that of a broad base – was very well adapted to mass financing. But it was principally an intermediation model, where credit was based on metal, but assets were converted 'into paper'. On these three points, the Reform was advantageous, notably through the guarantee it provided to these assets. Given the amounts involved, it could be said that a de facto monopoly was being attributed to it.

This was, in any case, what events after the Reformation indicated. The 11 months following its implementation would be marked: (1) by the failure of the 'run' on the Bank of England, probably organised by the Goldsmiths, and which would be illustrated by a successful capital increase, (2) by the failure of the Land Bank, despite its political support, and finally (3) the strengthening of relations with the Treasury, which from its point of view signalled a stronger position on the market.

(4) But the most significant was, of course, the reform of 1697, with the granting of those two monopolies which would allow the Bank to stabilise itself, giving it the issuing monopoly which led to its success (see Chapter 1).

At this point, however, the discussion must be curtailed.

Since it is recognised that the strength of these future banknotes[27] was linked to the Bank's resolve to support its bills with metal – and therefore with the new money – it can be said henceforth that the form of this decision was that of a *partnership* in which monetary policy and finance now complemented each other. This is why

> ==> today's Central Bank was born at that moment.

Consequently, this will make up the conclusion of this work. For its purpose was extremely precise. It was to highlight a philosopher's contribution to the institution of the first Central Bank. So, what has just been demonstrated is that the monetary reform that he led had in fact forged the link between money and credit. Hence, it was on this link that the Bank of England was able to establish itself.

==> A more effective contribution could not have been imagined

This is why the time has come to part with Locke. For it must be realised that these events almost marked the end of his public action. The facts are well known and his letters testify this[28]: he would publish the text as requested by Somers and adopted in substance by the government (October/November 1695), and ensured a vote for the monetary reform in Parliament (January 1696). He had then to fight for its implementation while failing to impose this famous transitory 'circulation at weight'. Finally, he oversaw the re-publication of his works (July 1696), as if it was his last contribution. Indeed, the reform was effectively implemented and became irrevocable when the new Parliament confirmed it (October 1696).

But then, Locke remained silent, namely, on this Bank Reform, and it will be necessary to question this matter. In fact, he only reconsidered these monetary affairs once, sticking to the simple status of a man of influence which he strove to remain. He passed away several years later.

This Reform was, therefore, the peak of his action, the action of one of some great philosophers who can be said to have founded our democracies.

Thus, this essay has attempted to illustrate how Locke accomplished this work.

Notes

1 'He *strictly defined money as gold and silver*' (Op. cit., p. 55). This interpretation is consistent with its truncated reading of the status of pledge discussed in Chapter 5.

2 'Locke acknowledges that people...accept lightweight coin...in ordinary transactions', Carey in '*Locke's philosophy...*', pp. 14–15.

3 See also this argument: '*no wonder if the price and value of things be...incertain, when the measure itself is lost*' (FC-33).

4 Ricardo, *Principles of political economy*, Chapter II.

5 Traditional measurement – which was still that of Galileo – started from an intuitive ontology to assume that movement was measured by real entities (the foot, the thumb, etc.). It referred to that of the metallists and was mistakenly attributed to Locke. Newton's measurement was ontologically different. He argued that space was the first reality – like a Kant '*a priori*' – and therefore required a convention which would become later 'the standard meter' (see Koyré [1966,1973]).

6 To complete the comparison with physics, this standpoint referred to the notion of simultaneity (Essay-LII-ChXV-§8).

7 This was probably not the case of 'the poor', as was too often stated, who lived largely outside of the monetised economy at the time.

8 Hutchinson, '*The emergence of political economy: 1662/1776*', 1988; Eltis, '*Locke... and the establishment of a sound money*', 1995; Hawtrey, '*Currency and credit*', 1927. Horsefield was more careful.

9 Feavearyear, '*The pound sterling*', 1963, p. 135.

10 In a recent article, Kleer summarised the available data on price movements. It appears that the significant developments for this discussion refer only to the period mid-1695 to mid-1696. They reflect the phenomenon of flight from money discussed in the box: '*For non-agricultural prices, the index [calculated by Horsefield] hovers near 101 (Ap 1694), then near 97 to July 1695, jumps to 102 in August,...then to a peak of 113.8 (Ap 1696)...to 104 (June) and near 102 for the rest of the year...For 12 agricultural products...an index calculated by Li –* and adjusted to the former - *stands near 115 for most of 1694, falls after the...harvest...to 93 (June, July 1695)...climbs to 124.9 (May 1696) and...progressively back to 110.2 (Dec 1696)*', in '*Reappraising Locke's case...*', 2001, pp. 3,4.

11 For this notion, refer to note 38 in Chapter 1.

12 Notice that for cartalism – which many of these authors claim to be their own – it is *the law* and not *usage* that confers 'extrinsic' value on the unit of account.

13 See Macaulay, Op. cit., p. 702.

14 '*The distributive aspects of the recoinage are generally ignored by modern commentators*', (Op. cit., p. 545).

15 See Appleby's surprising statement: '*coins...were not hoarded as Gresham's Law would have it*' (Op. cit., p. 46).

16 Caffentzis blamed these commentators for their inability to integrate the action '*of the others – clippers, counterfeiters*'. He is perfectly right...even if the argument could be also used against him, in so far as he ignored hoarding – see Chapter 5.

17 Kelly mentions, in particular, the proposal made in 1698 by Locke and three protagonists of the 'board of trade', intended to counter the resumption of

gold/silver arbitrage (it was a question of lowering the public price of gold to 21 s – 6 p). The proposal had little effect on cross-border gold/silver transfers.

18 Kelly includes here the downward trend in the price of gold in 1696.

19 This point refers notably to Bodin's theory, which was widely accepted at the time – see Chapter 5 note 18.

20 Lowndes anticipated it (Op. cit., pp. 85–86), but confused the effects of the new reliability of money and the increase of par value.

21 To be comprehensive, the probable *deterioration* in the balance of payments should be added – and not an improvement as it is often believed – due to the inversion of the terms of trade and the deterioration in British positions. The price effects would only have been long term.

22 Total cost for the State is estimated – in numerary – to £2.7 million, and the loss of individuals to £1 million.

23 Op. cit., pp. 695,731.

24 In '*a contribution to the critique…*', 1904, p. 94.

25 Locke's entire standpoint was as follows: it accepted the principle of compensation to individuals and the principle of a tax for State losses. But the balance was unlikely to be achieved '*without anybody's loss*'. And '*too much care…of particulars endangers the whole*' (FC-104, 105).

26 On tallies at 6%. The discount rate was −21% in March 1695. From Dickson (Op. cit., p. 347).

27 Which, strictly speaking, appeared in 1745 (as anonymous bearer notes). The amount of bearer notes went from £1.3 million in 1698 to £2.2 million (1721) and £4.1 million (1741), in Coppieters [1955].

28 Notably, letters of 6, 24, 28 April and 3 May 1696.

Conclusion
The first step towards democracy

Our democratic societies are institutionalised societies, and the understanding of their institutions is essential to their stability. But an institution cannot be addressed like a simple organisation. It can only really be comprehended based on its origins, in other words, from the missions assigned to it and their inclusion in those of the State. So, if Locke's relations with the Bank of England have been chosen here for investigation, it is above all for this reason. It was a question of measuring how a preeminent philosopher – reputed to be linked to this future institution – had contributed to thinking out those missions.

However, the final stage of this work has been reached and it can be affirmed that this choice was justified. For although the economist Locke has often been studied, mainly because of his reputation, it cannot be said that there is a real consensus – even partial – on his writings. So, this choice enabled a fresh approach to his work and, in particular, his address to Parliament – 'Some Considerations'. It is then possible to confirm that these writings not only participated in the decisions that established the Bank of England, but also contributed to giving them their meaning: and this as much through the topic of 'banking regulation' which shed light on the origin of its creation, as through this 'content guarantee' of money which was at the core of the Monetary Reform. These are positions that must be interpreted in relation to each other, since the heart of the Bank of England's project was in the monetary anchoring of its credit policy. They affirm, above all, Locke's involvement in the choices linked to this creation.

But the main result of this work is undoubtedly elsewhere, and it answers this problem of understanding that has been weighing on the interpretation of Locke for such a long time. It stems from the difficulty at the time of Locke in conceptualising the very instruments of this future institution – money and credit – and which made it impossible to already anticipate these decisions. Therefore, this work has determined that it was

Locke who had to assume it. But he did so as a philosopher, precisely as a philosopher of Natural Right, which means that he knew how to assign these money and credit to *identifiable* practices, such as the use of metal as a tool for arbitration. But practices that were so well *accepted* that they could be set as *norms*, namely, both as *legal rules* and *a foundation for law*.

It is this term, 'both', that is the essence of his thinking.

On the one hand, it enabled him to decide on legitimate practices in monetary and financial matters, which explained the care Locke took in delineating the different types of speculation. But, more importantly, he could derive from them the very laws that would guarantee them, which then became confused with these famous decisions. From there on, the essence of his contribution can be summarised in three points.

1. It starts from a reconsideration of money, which can now be described as *abstraction* and *dualism*. Since where money was still thought of as a material object, and very often as a commodity, for Locke it would become a duality: 'money' becoming a purely political object – the abstract object of monetary policy – but which would depend on metal, which therefore remains its primary element. But this metal – and this is where the financial dimension of money appears – would receive an innovative status. It would become a pledge, an object which is generally defined as a guarantee for a loan, and which here was confused with the very function of a store of value.

The basis of his standpoint would then be that this pledge status was the result of a 'general consent', which meant that it was the norm for all transactions. For this reason, he spoke of the humanity.

2. However, there was a logic to this position, which stipulated the practices that this pledge legitimised – the most important being the dynamic *of saving* – leading to a real market for land ownership capital, but also the *practice of lending*.

Hence, *the turning point is that because of this legitimisation, Locke was able to conceive credit for what it really was – a contract –* but with a *purpose* and a purpose of *general interest*: to reinvest savings in the economy.

3. With those consequences that clarify its support for the Bank of England. (1) As on the one hand, this vision ratified the intermediary role that the bank demanded, and which made it possible to lay down the principles of banking regulation: in short, principles being an optimal transformation of savings. But on the other hand, it made

it possible to determine (2) the monetary policy of a State whose responsibility evolved into guaranteeing this relationship between money and pledge – to be precise: guaranteeing its metal content; (3) but also its link to credit, which would correspond to maintaining the money's par value.

So, it is the combination of these three points that shapes the result of this work. Since collectively they infer that Locke had taken a founding approach, both financially and institutionally: *the establishment, based on a reliable money of a regulated financial system.*

He provided the intellectual rationale for this.

If this idea is acknowledged, then the consequences in terms of interpretation and of its recurrent difficulties should also be acknowledged. For the fact is that, apart from a few exceptions, none of Locke's interpreters have been able to reproduce these two essential dimensions of his thinking: the latter being more often confined to a conservative approach, a simple market theory concerning interest, or a simple metallist one concerning money. Locke has even been accused of being ignorant of the principle of a monetary policy, following the example of Appleby and the majority of his interpreters in the last century. This obviously raises questions because it is rare to observe such incomprehension disparity in the field of economics. But this work has been able to show that it was not an error in the way it is intuitively perceived, but a *problem of method.* This stemmed from this bias which was to refute any philosophical dimension to economic analysis – in other words, any normative approach to these topics.

However, the unrealistic nature of such behaviour is now obvious. For at the time, it was not possible to adopt even a reflexive attitude to money or credit without addressing the question of their finality and *trust* in them. This could only be a philosophical question, because it referred to the question of the law and, above all, its *legitimacy*: it means *the very essence* of political power. In any case, it is sufficient to explain the presence of a philosopher in such a process. Consequently, it is from this perspective that these authors should be answered: that these questions on trust, finality and legitimacy were an integral part of the process of creating the Bank of England and which is also called 'the financial revolution'. Hence, the success of this revolution – a success that has been palpable since the turn of the century – comes from the fact that these questions were dealt in-depth.

This is ultimately the meaning behind Locke's action and contribution.

But conversely, this success also encompasses the main *criticism* that can be levelled at the economist Locke. It would be wrong, at the end of this work, not to mention that point. For if this discussion is henceforth put into perspective it will be observed that the financial policies – of which he authorised the implementation – immediately generated major changes in both monetary and financial practices – for instance, the somewhat rapid use of the Bank of England notes as bank clearing tools, or on another level, the substitution of gold for silver. The question to be asked is how Locke could have pre-empted them.

Yet to re-read Locke in this way also means admitting real weaknesses. A typical example is gold, where he failed to see its growing importance in transactions. But more generally, it can be stated that he only knew how to analyse the field he was in contact with, and without ever projecting himself into a future world. Two examples will be provided here to prove this.

This will, first of all, be determined through his personal notes taken on the management of the Bank of England and, in particular, on its risk management. They testify to Locke's concern about the rule of public disclosure of accounts which the Bank had adopted in a premonitory way. In particular, this passage:

> A great treasure heaped to gather in view may make many people fingers itch.[1]

Even if the facts concurred with him – the first 'run' on the Bank was based on the credence of such information – this was indeed a *conservative* attitude. Or, to put it another way, it reflected a disparity that was beginning to widen between an essentially moral discourse – focused on behaviour – and the future world, much more linked to objective mechanisms and sensitive to factual data.

But the best example is the question of the status of the Bank of England, and the difficulty Locke had in conceiving this. It could be analysed through the reform of 1697, and the silence he adopted on the subject. For even if it was only a temporary decision, it can be considered that it was on this occasion that the Bank of England acquired its status as a State Institution: this being due not only to the monopolies granted to it, but above all, to the stabilisation of its relationship with the State.

So, it might be considered that this clarification satisfied one of Locke's major concerns about the Bank. For it testified both the power of Parliament and the Bank's independence from government – or rather, to its anchoring in the economy. These are principles that he had put forward, and his silence, therefore, seems to have been only a reflection of his (very real) desire to withdraw from public life.

This is not so straightforward. Since the problem posed by this reform was broader than the issues through which it was approached – in this case State short-term financing. It was in the end to establish the Bank over the long term, in other words, to imbed it into the general interest – while maintaining its commercial status. This signified an objective, not just a qualitative, conceptualisation of this interest, referring here to the balance between financing of the debt and the economy. But how far should the State be involved in debt? However, it is highly debateable that Locke had the means to conceive this. So, it has been stated in this work that, for him, public intervention was confused with the *interplay of norms and law*, and his vision of regulation was mainly moral. It was 'only' a question of ensuring a fair transfer of savings to the economy. It was certainly enough to conceive the Bank's mission and, therefore, the framework of an institution, but not to conceive everyday action – at least not in the long run.

Thus, leaving this silence aside, the following observation can surely be affirmed: *at the very moment when the financial system he defended was being established, Locke was reaching his own limits.*

Obviously, in terms of the points already discussed, these were only accessory aspects. But this disparity now seems meaningful. It is directly related to the issue that generally wraps up an essay on the history of ideas: that of Locke's intellectual filiation or, in other words, how it resounded in economic thinking. In this respect, there is a real paradox.

Since Locke is an author who has had a huge influence on European thinking, particularly on political philosophy. Yet – this has just been proven – this influence extended beyond ideas to a State's institution, and a State that would be a model for democracy. It would, moreover, be a long-term influence since the principles that were implemented would be applied for a very long time – whether with the gold standard or with financial policies to defend savings. It could therefore be imagined that the resonance encountered by Locke was expanded in economic thinking.

Paradoxically, however, this was not the case, and Schumpeter[2] is right on this point. In fact, there is no notable school of thought in economics that has been inspired by the economist Locke, even though 'Locke-the-philosopher' had a notable influence on the neoclassical authors. With hindsight, a sort of disengagement can in contrast be observed, an increasing strangeness between his moral conceptions and the world of economic theory. It is well known, moreover, that over the next two centuries this theory has been characterised by a poor financial approach and even by the survival of monetary metallism. Locke was in a totally different world.

However, this can be seen above all through Locke's comparison with early liberalism – that of Smith and Ricardo – and this work may be concluded on this point. For it is a recurring question for Locke's interpretation – as witnessed with many critics – but one that is too often posed in a biased way: by ignoring that the essential element in this comparison must be *the moral dimension of economic analysis*. From this point of view, however, the question is very easy to determine, and it leads to a twofold differentiation:

1. That of *economic doctrine*, which means judgements about practices and behaviour.

In this respect there is more than a kinship between Locke and the liberals, whatever his 'mercantilist' sympathies may have been. Since the essence of liberalism is not the principle of market freedom – largely understood long before Locke (Schumpeter) – but the free use of capital. It is the fact that collective wealth – the 'wealth of Nations' – depended, in his opinion, on the dynamics of private investment. It is necessary to be a Marxist on this point.

Yet, whatever it is called, it is *that idea* that has been observed in Locke: the justification for this dynamic and the will to steer it in a collective way – there is no other reason for his involvement in the financial revolution. It is therefore inappropriate – as was the case sometimes – to set Locke against the liberal authors, even if this collective dimension became more subdued over time.

2. But classical liberalism was more than just that. It was a doctrine linked to a theory, but more than a theory, it sought to base *specific knowledge* on the economy.

In fact it is from this liberalism that the idea of economic science, and even social science, was born (Foucault and Strauss). However, this was made from a *revamped ontology* that could be considered as amoral, by defending the existence of an economic nature that could be knowable through 'economic *laws*'.

But in this case, this ontology must be seen as alien and even hostile to Locke's thinking. Hence, this is a direct criticism of L. Strauss. Since for Locke, there is admittedly a natural law which governs behaviour in the same way, apparently, as for the liberals. But, this is the *law of reason* and that has to be assumed *knowingly* by the stakeholders: whereas, on the contrary, economic law ignores their morality, but imposes itself on them. So, the finding that must be made behind the words is that it was the origin of this separation which was mentioned above, of this strangeness which has been encountered throughout this essay. In fact, *it started from Adam Smith onwards that economic knowledge was no longer able to converse with Locke*. It can even be said that it turned its back on him.

But, if such is the case, this lack of understanding cannot be elicited without a certain amount of concern.

Since the events that have been covered here go beyond the framework of the economy alone. They linked effectively the founder of political freedom to the first economic institution in our history. It can, therefore, be asserted in a straightforward manner that it was the first step towards democracy. So, the fact that it can no longer be recognised through Locke does not bode well.

This work was written in order to oppose that.

Notes

1 Quoted by Wennerlind (Op. cit., p.133).
2 '*There is no bridge between Locke and the...theories of today*' (Op. cit., p. 329).

Bibliography

Bibliographical note

The purpose of this essay is to restore the meaning of the positions taken by Locke during the financial revolution. It was a public debate, in which the philosopher was directly involved, thus testifying to the substance of his political and economic thinking. This is why – and against the current trend of interpretation – careful choice has been made to refer purely to Locke's public texts on these questions, waiving from this rule only in the conclusion. So, this was based on the following:

1. With regard to the main texts: in the 1696 edition – known as 'Churchill' edition – which contains Locke's original texts, with the exception of the first 'Considerations' that Locke slightly modified in substance (1). This choice was made because Locke's main amendment – in addition to a small passage on banks – provided decisive clarification on the *nature of money*. The context of this addendum, *in the midst* of the monetary reform, would leave in no doubt as to what was at stake.
2. With regard to the intermediate notes written in 1696: on the scientific edition entitled 'Locke on money'. Their content was incorporated into his 'Further Considerations'.
3. With regard to Locke's correspondence: solely on Locke's letter exchanges with the 'college' – his political friends – as they had a clear vocation and probably influenced these debates.

For the remainder of the bibliography – exhaustiveness being unattainable – this essay has attempted to rely on the most representative texts, both of Locke's contemporary currents of thought and of the positions taken by his interpreters. However, the interested reader is invited to go further.

(1) In order to facilitate any research based on the 'reprints' of this edition, the pages in each text have been referenced independently.

Locke's main texts

- J Locke – several papers relating to money, interest and trade, 1696, London, Churchill
    1. Some considerations upon lowering the interest of money and raising the value of money, in a letter sent to a member of parliament – identified as (SC)
    2. Short observations on a printed paper intituled: for encouraging the coining silver money in England and keeping it – (SO)
    3. Further considerations concerning raising on the value of money – (FC)
- J Locke – in *Locke on Money*, 2 vol., 1991, under the supervision of Kelly (texts included under in the 'Further Considerations'
    1. Guineas
    2. A paper given to sir Trumbull which was written at his request
    3. Proposition sent to the Lord Justices
    4. Answers to my lord Keepers queries)
- E S de Beer – *Correspondence of John Locke*, vols 4&5,1979, Oxford University press.
- J Locke – Two treatise of government, a critical edition by P Laslett, 1960, Cambridge University Press – (TCG).
- - Essai philosophique concernant l'entendement humain, transl. Coste, 1723, Amsterdam, Fac simile.
- J Locke – Some considerations upon lowering the interest …1st edition, 1692, London, Churchill.
- J Locke – Manuscripts médicaux, transl: under the supervision of Crignon, in *Locke médecin*, Op. cit.

Other texts

- J Locke – Early writings on interest 1668–74, in *Locke on Money,* Op. cit.
- Venditio – 1695, in *Locke on Money*, Op. cit.
- J Locke – Essai sur la loi de Nature, transl. Guineret, 1986, Caen, Centre de philosophie politique
    - Epistolia de tolerantia, transl. Le Clerc,1992,Paris, Garnier-Flammarion
    - Some thoughts concerning education, transl. Compayré, 2007, Paris,Vrin
    - The reasonableness of Christianity, transl. Coste, 1740, Amsterdam, Fac Simile
- E S de Beer – Correspondence of John Locke, 8 vols., Op. cit.

General bibliography

Aglietta, M. (2002) *Whence and whiter money?,* The Future of Money, OECD.
Andreades, A. (1966) *History of the Bank of England,* 2 vol, New York, Kelly, reprint.

Appleby, J. (1976) *Locke, liberalism and the natural law,* Past & presen, Oxford University Press, no. 71, pp. 43–69.

Appleby, J. (1978) *Economic thought and ideology in 17th century,* Princeton University Press.

Asgill, J. (2018) *Several assertions in order to create another species of money,* Gale ecco-reprint.

Ashcraft, R. (1986) *Revolutionary politics and Locke's two treatise of government, Political theory,* Princeton University Press.

Ashcraft, R. (1968) Locke's state of nature: historical fact or moral fiction, American Political Science Review, vol. 62, no. 3.

Barbon, N. (1690) *A discourse of trade,* London, Milbourn.

Barbon, N. (1696) *A discourse concerning coining the money lighter, in answer to M Locke consideration,* London, Chiswell

Baxter, S. (1957) *The development of the Teasury,* Cambridge, Harvard University Press.

Bentham, J. (1780) *An introduction to the principles of moral and legislation,* New York, M Mack, reprint.

Berthoud, A. (1988) *Morale et enrichissement monétaire,* Economie et sociétés, no. 9.

Blanc, J. & Desmedt, L. (2019*) Les pensées monétaires dans l'histoire,* Paris, Garnier.

Blaug, M. (1964) *Economic theory in retrospect,* London, Heinemann.

Blaug, M. (1991) *The later mercantilist, Child and Locke,* Aldershot, Elgar.

Blaug, M. (1991) *The early mercantilist, Mun,* Misselden, de Malynes, Aldershot, Elgar.

Blaug, M. (1995) *The quantity theory of money,* Aldershot, Elgar.

Bloch, O. R. (1971) *La philosophie de Gassendi, nominalisme, matérialisme, métaphysique,* La Haye, Nijhoff.

Bodin, J. (1593) *Réponse au paradoxe de M Malestroit,* in *les six livres de la République,* Lyon, Vincent.

Von Böhm-Bawerk, E. (1902) *Histoire critique des théories de l'intérêt du capital,* trad. Bernard, Paris, Giard.

Bohun, E. (1696) *The proposal for raising of the silver coin,* Text online.

Bonar, J. (1893) *Philosophy and political economy in some of their historical relations,* London, Sonnenschein.

Bouillot, C. (2019) *The conflict in the Lockean State of Nature,* Journal of the Economic Thought, vol. 41, no. 4.

Bourne, H. R. (1876) *The life of John Locke,* London, King, fac simile.

Braudel, F. (1979) *Civilisation matérielle, économie et capitalisme, TII: XVème-XVIIIème,* Paris, Colin.

Bredin, J. D. (1988) *Siéyes, la clé de la Révolution Française,* Saint-Amand, Fallois.

Briscoe, J. (1696) *A discourse on the late fund of the Million-act…Lottery-Act and Bank of England,* London, Bell

Caffentzis, G. (1989) *Clipped coins, abused words and civil government: John Locke's philosophy of money,* New York, Autonomedia Press.

Caffentzis, G. (2003) *Medical metaphors and monetary strategies in the political economy of Locke and Berkeley,* History of Political Economy, vol. 35, no. 5.

Caffentzis, G. (2008) *John Locke, thee philosopher of prime accumulation,* Bristol, Radical Pamphleteer #5

Carey, D. & Finlay, C. (2007) *The empire of credit*, Dublin, Irish Academy Press.

Carey, D. (2011) *John Locke money and credit in 'the empire of credit'*, Op. cit.

Carey, D. (2013) *Locke's species, money and philosophy*, Annals of Science, no. 70 (3), pp.357-80.

Carey, D. (2014) *Locke's philosophy of money*, in *Money and political economy in the Enlighment*, Oxford, Voltaire Foundation.

Carruthers, B. G. (1999) *City of capital: politics and markets in the English financial revolution*, Princeton University Press.

Cary, J. (1696) *An essay on the coin and the credit of England*, Text online.

Chalk, A. F. (1951) *Natural law and the rise of economic individualism in England*, Journal of Political Economy, no. 59.

Challis, C. E. (1992) *History of the English Mint*, Cambridge University Press.

Chandaman, C. D. (1975) *The English public revenue, 1660-1688*, Oxford University Press.

Chevallier, J. J. (1983) *Histoire des idées politiques*, Paris, Editions Sciences Po.

Child, J (1754) *A discourse about Trade wherein the reduction of money is recommended*, transl. de Gournay, Amsterdam, Neaulmes.

Child, J. (1698) *A new discourse on trade*, London, Sowle.

Clapham, J, H. (1944) *The Bank of England: a history*, Cambridge University Press.

Clement, S. (1696) *A dialogue between a country gentleman and a merchant*, Text online.

Coleman, W. O. (2000) *The significance of John Locke medical studies for his economic thought*, History of Political Economy, vol. 32, no.4.

Collins, M. (1993) *Central banking in history*, Aldershot, Elgar.

Cook, T. (1936) *History of political philosophy*, New York, Prentice Hall.

Coppieters, E. (1955) *English banknote circulation*, Université Catholique Louvain.

Cox, R. H. (1960) *Locke on war and peace*, Oxford University Press.

Craig, J. (1946) *Newton at the mint*, Cambridge University Press.

Crignon, C. (2016) *Locke médecin*, Paris, Garnier.

Culpeper, T. (1754) (o) *Treatise against usury*, in *A discourse about Trade...*, transl. de Gournay, Op. cit.

Culpeper, T. (y) (1670) *The necessity of abatting usury re-asserted*, Text online.

Dang, A. T. (1997) *Monnaie, Libéralisme et Cohésion Sociale*, Revue Economique, vol. 48, no. 3.

Davenant, C. (1942) *Two manuscripts 1/a memorial concerning coin, 2/a memorial concerning credit*, Baltimore, John Hopkins, reprint.

Desmedt, L. (2007) *Les fondements monétaires de la "révolution financière" anglaise*, in *La monnaie dévoilée par ses crises*, Paris, Editions EHESS.

Diatkine, D. & Bouillot, C. (2017) *Le système de la liberté naturelle... qui sont les adversaires d'A. Smith?*, Cahier économie politique vol. 2, no73.

Diatkine, D. (1986) *De la convention à l'illusion*, Thèse: Université Paris 1.

Diatkine, D. (1988) *La monnaie dans la philosophie politique de John Locke*, Economie et Sociétés, *Oeconomia*, no. 3.

Dickson, P. G. (1967) *Financial revolution in England: a study in the development of public credit*, London, MacMillan.

Diemer, A. & Guillemin, H. (2009) *Locke: De l'état de nature à la 'société économique'*, *Cahiers d'économie politique, Juil 2009*.

Diemer, A. & Guillemin, H. (2011) *La place du travail dans la pensée lockienne* – in C. Lavialle, *Regards croisés sur le travail*, Presses Universitaires Orléans.

Dunn, J. (1967) *Consent in the political theory of Locke*, The Historical Journal, vol. 10, no. 2.

Dunn, J. (1968) *Justice and the interpretation*, Political Studies, vol. 16, no. 1

Dunn, J. (1969) *The political thought of Locke*, Cambridge University Press.

Dunn, J. (1981) *Locke economist and social scientist by K Vaughn*, The American Historical Review, vol. 86, no. 2.

Eich, S. (2018) *John Locke and the politics of monetary depoliticization*, Princeton University Press, working paper.

Eltis, W. (1995) *Locke, the quantity theory of money, and the establishment of a sound money*, in *The Quantitative Theory of Money*, Blaug, Op. cit.

Fay, C. R. (1933) *Locke versus Lowndes*, Cambridge Historical Journal, vol. 4, no. 2.

Feavearyear, A. E. (1932) *The pound: history of British money*, Oxford University Press.

Forster, G. (2005) *John Locke's politics of moral consensus*, Cambridge University Press.

Foucault, M. (2002) *The order of things*, transl. Tavistock/Routledge, London, Routledge

Francis, J. H. (1888) *History of the Bank of England*, London, Willoughby.

Garo, I. (2000) *Monnaie et richesse chez J Locke*, Revue de Synthèse, série no. 4, no. 1&2.

Godfrey, M. (1995) *A short account of the Bank of England*, in *Francis: history of the Bank*. Op. cit.

Goldie, M. (1992) *J Locke's circle and James II*, The Historical Journal, vol. 35, no. 3

Gonnard, R. (1935/36) *Histoire des doctrines monétaires dans ses rapports avec l'histoire des monnaie*, Paris, Sirey.

Goyard-Fabre, S. (1992) *La propriété dans la philosophie Politique de Locke*, Archives de philosophie (4), Faculté jésuite de Paris.

Goyard-Fabre, S. (1994) *Pufendorf et le droit naturel*, Paris, P.U.F.

Grampp, W. D. (1981) *The controversy upon usury in the 17th*, Journal of European Economic History, no. 10, pp. 671-95.

Grassby, R. (1969) *The rate of profit in the 17th*, English Historical Review, no. 84, pp. 721-51.

Grassby, R. (1999) *The idea of capitalism before the industrial revolution*, New York, Rowman.

Grey, A. (1769) *Debates of the House of Commons, from…1667 to…1694*, London, Henry.

Grotius, H. (2011) *Le droit de la guerre et de la Paix*, trad. Barbeyrac, Presses Universitaires de Caen, fac simile.

Habakkuk, H. (1952) *The long-term rate of interest and the price of Land in the 17th*, Economic History Review, vol 5. no 1.

Harpham, E. J. (1984) *Natural law and early liberal economic though*, Social Science Quartery, vol. 65, no. 4.

Harrisson, J. & Laslett, P. (1965) *The library of John Locke*, Oxford University Press.

Hartog, G. D. (1990) *Tully's Locke*, Political Theory, vol. 18, no. 4.

Hawtrey, R. G. (1927) *Currency and credit*, London, Longmans.

Hazard, P. (1935) *La crise de la conscience européenne*, Paris, Boivin.

Hegeland, T. (1951) *The quantitative theory of money*, Göteborg, Elanders.

Heidegger, M. (1983) *Le principe de raison*, trad. Preau, Paris, Gallimard.

Hekscher, E. (1955) *Mercantilism,* 2 vol, London, Allen and Unwinn.

Helm, P. (1973) *Locke on Faith and Knowledge*, The Philosophical Quarterly, vol. 23, no. 90.

Henry, J. (1999) *John Locke, property rights and economic theory*, Journal of Economic Issues, vol. 33, no. 3.

Hicks, J. (1937) *Mr Keynes and the classics, a suggested interpretation*, Econometrica, no. 2.

Hill, C. & Postan, M. (1977) *Histoire économique et sociale de la Grande-Bretagne, T1: des origines au 18ème siècle*, transl. Bertrand, Paris, Seuil.

Hobbes, T. (1999) *Leviathan*, transl. Tricaud, Paris, Dalloz.

Hobbes, T. (1982) *Elementa philosophica de Cive*, transl. Sorbière, Paris, GF.

Hodges, J. (1697) *The present state of England as to coin and publick charges*, London, Bell.

Horsefield, J. K. (1960) *British monetary experiments*, Cambridge, Harvard University Press.

Horsefield, J. K. (1956) *Inflation and Deflation in 1694-1696*, Economica, vol 23, no. 91, pp. 229-243.

Houblon, J. (1690) *Observations on the bill against the exportation of Gold and silver*, in *House of Lords 1690/91*, Text online.

Hundert, E. J. (1972) *The making of Homo Faber: John Locke between ideology and history*, Journal of the History of Ideas, vol. 33, no 1.

Hutchinson, T. W. (1988) *Before A Smith, the emergence of political economy: 1662/ 1776*, Oxford, Blackwell.

Irvine, R. (2009) *Labor and commerce in Locke and early 18th century...*, Johns Hopkins University Press, vol. 76, no. 4.

Kant, I. (1985) *Prolégomènes à toute métaphysique future qui pourra se présenter comme science*, in Oeuvres, trad. Rivelaygue, Paris, Gallimard.

Kant, I. (1985) *Was ist Aufklärung?*, trad. Wismann, In Oeuvres Op. cit.

Keirn, T. & Melton, F. (1990) *Thomas Manley and the rate-of-interest debate*, Journal of British Studies, vol. 29, no. 2.

Kelly, P. (1991) *Locke on money*, 2 Vol., *Introduction*, Oxford, Clarendon Press.

Kelly, P. (1988) *All things richly to enjoy: economics and politics in Locke's two treatises of government*, Political Studies, vol. 36, no. 2.

Kelly, P. (1969) *A note on Locke's pamphlets on money*, Cambridge Bibliographical Society, vol. 5, no 1.

Kendall, W. (1965) *Locke and the doctrine of the majority rule*, Chicago, University of Illinois Press.

Keynes, J. M. (1991) *The general theory of employment, interest and money*, London, Mac Millan.

Kleer, R. (2004) *The ruin of their "Diana", Lowndes, Locke and the bankers*, History of The Political Economy, vol. 36, no. 3.

Kleer, R. (2001) *Reappraising Locke's case against "raising the coin"*, University of Regina, working paper.

Koyre, A. (1966) *Etudes Galiléennes*, Paris, Hermann.

Koyre, A. (1973) *From the closed world to the infinite universe*, transl. Tar, Paris, Gallimard.

Laslett, P. (1960) *J Locke: two treatises critical edition*, Cambridge University Press.

Laslett, P. (1957) *J Locke, the great recoinage and the origins of the board of trade; 1695-1698*, The Williams and Mary Quarterly, vol. 14, no. 3.

Laslett, P. (1965) *The world we have lost*, London, Methuen.

Law, J. (1705) *Money and trade considered*, Edinburgh, Text online.

Le Branchu, J. H. (1934) *Ecrits notables sur la monnaie*, 2T, Paris, PUF.

Leigh, A. H. (1974) *John Locke and the quantity theory of money* in Blaug, *The Later Mercantilists*, Op.cit.

Leibniz, G. F. (1986) *Nouveaux essais sur l'entendement humain*, éditeur Boutroux, Paris, Delagrave.

Letwin, W. (1963) *The origins of scientific economics, English Economic Thought*, London, Methuen.

Von Leyden, W. (1954) *John Locke: essays on the law of nature*, Oxford University Press.

Li, M. H. (1963) *The Great Recoinage of 1696 to 1699*, London, Weidenfeld.

Lowndes, W. (1695) *Report concerning an essay for the amendment of the silver coins*, London.

Macaulay, T. (1855) *History of England from the accession of James II*, 5 vol., London, Longman.

Mac Culloch, J. R. (1856) *A select collection of scarce and valuable tracts on money*, London, Online.

Macpherson, C. B. (1951) *Locke on capitalist appropriation*, Western Political quarterly, vol. 4, no. 4.

Macpherson, C. B. (1954) *The social bearing of Locke's political theory*, Western Political Quarterly, vol. 7, no. 1.

Macpherson, C. B. (1990) *The political theory of possessive individualism*, Oxford University Press.

Malynes, G. (1623) *The center of the circle of commerce, a refutation of a treatise intituled the circle of commerce*, London, W Iones, reprint.

Manley, T. (1669) *Usury at 6 per cent examined*, London, Ratcliffe.

Marx, K. (1887) *Capital*, transl. Moore, London, Sonnenschein.

Marx, K. (1904) *Contribution to the critique of political economy*, transl. Stone, Chicago, Kerr.

Marx, K. (1976) *Theorien über den mehrwert*, trad. (sous la direction de), G. Badia, Paris, Editions Sociales.

Mayhew, N. (2012) *Silver in England 1600-1800*, in *Money in the Preindustrial World*, J Munro, London, Pickering.

Mill, J. S. (1889) *Utilitarianism*, transl. Le Monnier, Paris, Alcan.

Misselden, E. (1971) *The circle of commerce or the balance of trade*, New York, Kelley.

Mitchell, B.R. (1962) *Abstract of British historical statistics*, Cambridge University Press.

Mitchell, N. (1986) *J. Locke and the rise of capitalism, History of the political economy*, Duke University Press, vol. 18, no. 2.

Monroe, A. E. (1923) *Monetary theory before A Smith*, Cambridge University Press.

Mun, T. (1621) *A discourse of trade to the East Indies*, London.

Neale, T. (1696) *A proposal for amending the silver coins of England*, London, Baldwin.

Newton, I. (1985) *Principia mathematica philosophiae naturalis*, trad. Biarnais, Paris, C. Bourgois.

North, D. (1907) *Discourses upon trade*, Baltimore, John Hopkins, reprint.

North, D. & Weingast, B. (1989) *Constitution and commitment: the evolution of institutions…in 17th*, The Journal of Economic History, 1989, vol. 49, no. 4.

Nozick, R. (2016) *Anarchy, state and utopia*, transl. d'Auzac, Paris, PUF.

Olivecrona, K. (1974) *Locke's theory of appropriation*, The Philosophical Quarterly, vol. 24, no. 96.

Onur, U. I. (2011) *Enclosing in God's name, accumulating for mankind*, the Review of Politics, vol. 73, no. 1.

Ormazabal, K. (2007) *Lowndes and Locke on the value of money*, Ikerlanak, working paper.

Paterson, W. (1993) *A brief account of the intended Bank of England*, in Collins, Central Banking and History, Op. cit.

Petty, W. (1906) *Treatise of taxes and contributions*, in *Œuvres 2T*, transl. Dussauze, Giard et Brière.

Petty, W. (1906) *Quantulumcunque concerning money*, in Œuvre, Op. cit.

Petty, W. (1906) *Political arithmetick*, in Œuvres, Op. cit.

Pincus, S. (2009) *1988: The First Modern Revolution*, New Haven, Yale University Press.

Plamenatz, J. (1996) *Man and society: From the Middle Ages to Locke*, London, Longman.

Pocock, J. G. (1980) *The myth of John Locke and the obsession with Liberalism*, in Papers Read at the Clark Library Seminar, UCLA.

Pocock, J. G. (1998) *Virtue, Commerce and History, Essay on political thought in history, chiefly in the 18th century*, transl. H. Aji, Paris, PUF.

Polin, R. (1960) *La politique morale de John Locke*, Paris, P.U.F.

Potter, W. (2010) *The key of wealth*, Nabu Press, reprint.

Pribram, K. (1986) *Les fondements de la pensée économique*, trad. Bertrand, Paris, Economica.

Pufendorf, S. (1721) *On the law of nature and nations*, transl. Kenneth, London, Walthoe.

Quinn, S. (1996) *Gold, Silver and the Glorious Révolution: arbitrage between Bills and Bullions*, Journal of Economic History, vol. 49, no 3.

Rand, B. (1927) *The correspondence of Locke and Clarke*, Oxford University Press.

Ricardo, D. (1951) *On the principles of political economy and taxation*, in *Ricardo, works and correspondence*, Cambridge University Press, fac simile.

Ricardo, D. (1824) *Plan for the establishment of a national Bank*, in Andréades, Op. cit.

Rist, C. (1951) *Histoire des doctrines relatives au crédit et à la monnaie*, Paris, Sirey.

Roche, C. (1992) *La connaissance et la loi dans la pensée économique libérale (classique)*, Thèse, Paris, L'Harmattan.

Rodocanachi, L. (1933) *La philosophie de Locke et la crise monétaire anglaise*, Académie des sciences morales et politiques, no. 2.

Van Roey, E. (1905) *La monnaie d'après St Thomas*, Revue néoscolastique, Louvain, 12ème année, no. 45.

Rogers, T. (2001) *The 9 first years of the Bank of England*, Oxford, Clarendon, fac simile.

Rubini, D. (1985) *Politics and the battle of the bank 1688/97*, English Historical Review, vol. 85, no. 70.

Rubini, D. (1968) *Court and the country 1688/1702*, London, Rupert Hart Davis.

Russel, D. (2004) *Locke on land and labor*, Philosophical Studies, vol. 117, no. 1/2.

Sabine, G.H. (1945) *A History of Political Theory*, New York, George Harrap.

Sachse, W. (1986) *Lord Somers: a political portrait*, Manchester University Press.

Sargent, T. & Velde, F. (2002) *The big problem of small change*, Princeton University Press.

Schumpeter, J. A. (1994) *History of economic analysis, T1*, London, Routledge, reprint.

Schumpeter, J. A. (2005) *Das Wesen des Geldes*, trad. Jaeger, Paris, L'harmattan.

Shackle, G. L. (1967) *The years of high theory, 1926-1939*, Cambridge University Press.

Shaw, W. A. (1896) *Select tracts and documents illustrative of English monetary history*, London, Cass.

Shirras, G. F. & Craig, J. H. (1945) *Sir Isaac Newton and the Currency*, The Economic Journal, vol. 55, no. 218/219.

Sigmund, P. E. (2005) *Waldron and the religious turn in Locke's scholarship*, Reviews of Politics, vol. 67, no. 3.

Simmons, J. (1992) *The Lockean theory of rights*, Princeton University Press.

Simmons, J. (1989) Locke's state of nature, *Political Theory*, vol. 17, no. 3.

Simmons, J. (1976) *Tacit consent and political obligation*, Philosophy & Public Affairs, vol. 5, no 3.

Skinner, Q. (1988) *Meaning and understanding in the theory of ideas*, in *Meaning and context*, Op. cit.

Smith, A. (1995) *An inquiry into the nature and the causes of the wealth of nations*, transl. Greenstein, Paris, P.U.F.

Spitz, F. (1986) *Le concept d'Etat de Nature chez Locke et Pufendorf*, Archives de philosophie, vol. 49, no. 3.

Spitz, F. (2001) *John Locke et les fondements de la liberté moderne*, Paris, P.U.F.

Spitz F. (1994) *Introduction au second traité de Gouvernement Civil*, Paris, P.U.F.

Steele, I. K. (1968) *Politics of colonial policy: the board of trade*, Oxford University Press.

Steuart, J. (1767) *An inquiry into principles of political economy*, London, Millar.

Stiglitz, J. E. & Weiss, A. (1981) *Credit rationing in markets with imperfect information*, American Economic Review, vol. 71, no. 3.

Strauss, L. (1953) *Natural right and history*, Chicago University Press.

Taieb, P. *Le jardin aux sentiers qui bifurquent* – www.taieb.net

Temple, R. (1696) *Short remarks about M Lock's book in answer M Lounds*, London, Baldwin, reprint. Theret, B. (2014) *Philosophies politiques de la monnaie: une comparaison de Hobbes, Locke et Fichte*, Oeconomia, vol 4, no. 4.

Tiran, A. (2012) *J Locke, Ecrits monétaires*, transl. Briozzo, Paris, Garnier

Tucker, G. S. (1960) *Progress and profits in British economic thought 1650-1850*, Cambridge University Press.

Tully, J. (1980) *A discourse on property: John Locke and his adversaries*, Cambridge University Press.

Tully, J. (1988) *Meaning and context*, Cambridge, Polity Press.

Tully, J. (1993) *An approach to political philosophy: Locke in contexts*, Cambridge University Press.

Vaughan, R. (1675) *A discourse of coin and coinage: The first invention, use, matter, forms, Proportions and Differences, ancient & moderns...*, London, Grayes.

Vaughn, K. (1980) *Locke as an economist and a social scientist*, Chicago University Press.

Viano, C. A. (1958*) I rapport tra Locke and Shawtesbury, e la teoria economische de Locke,* revista di filosofia, no. 69.

Vickers, D. (1960) *Studies in the theory of money*, London, Owen.

Vidonne, P. (1982) Nature, rente et travail, Thèse Paris I.

Viner, J. (1962) *Essay on the intellectual history of economics*, Princeton University Press.

Waldron, J. (1989) *John Locke: social contract versus political anthropology, The Review of Politics*, vol. 51, no. 1.

Weber, M. (1967) *Die protestantische ethic und der Geist des Kapitalismus,* trad. Chavy, Paris, Plon.

Wennerlind, C. (2011) *Casualties of credit*, Cambridge, Harvard University Press.

Wennerlind, C. (2004) *The death penalty as monetary policy: the practice and punishment of monetary crime*, History of Political Economy, vol. 36, no. 1.

Private file – *Comparison of the three versions of the 'Considerations'* (on demand).

Index